Murphy's:
25 Years of Recipes and Memories

Other books by Jan Butsch

*Just A Stage*

# Murphy's:
# 25 Years of Recipes and Memories

by
Tom Murphy and Jan Butsch

To T.R. Murphy
I hope you enjoy
the stories and the recipes
Best Regards!

Tom Murphy

Schroder Media

Schroder Media

Published by Schroder Media, LLC
1175 Peachtree Street, Suite 1812
Colony Square, Building 100
Atlanta, Georgia 30361
www.schrodermedia.com

Cover and book design: Heidi Rizzi
Copy and recipe editing: Brigit Binns
Recipe testing: Doris Koplin, Tony Laub
Copy editing: Blane Bachelor
Principal photography: Ralph Daniels
Additional photography: Reid Childers, Chris Schroder
Recipe index: Sharon Hilgenberg
People and Places index: Catherine Butsch

ISBN: 0-9762288-1-5

Library of Congress Control Number: 2005931373

Printed and bound in Korea
First printing, 2005

To my loving wife Susan,
who knows just when to throw the towel at me
without ever throwing the towel in.
*– Tom Murphy*


To my best friend and husband Chris,
who makes all things seem possible
and everything more fun.
*– Jan Butsch*

# Table of Contents

About Murphy's    1

Introduction    2

Wine Shop: Then and Now    6

Beginnings: "Hey, You're the Cheese Man!"    7

I'll Never Go Into the Restaurant Business    10

The High School Bleus    12

Market By Day, School By Night    13

The History of Virginia-Highland    16

A Neighborhood Waiting to Happen    18

Closed on Opening Day    20

Creating a Sense of Belonging    21

Early Press and Customer Feedback    25

Mixing Family and Business    28

A Bit o' the Green    31

From a Deli to a Restaurant: The First Coffee Mug    33

Hiring Talent    35

My Big, Fat Catering Disasters    42

Why I Will Never Go Back into Catering    45

The Murphy's Contest: It's in the Bag    46

A Moving Experience: How I Got My Gray Hair    47

Improving My Little Sandwich Shop    51

Tasting Trips    54

A Parade of Talent    55

| | |
|---|---|
| Lou Locricchio | 56 |
| Alon Balshan | 58 |
| Rob Atherholt | 59 |
| Gerry Klaskala | 62 |
| Shaun Doty | 65 |
| Michael Tuohy | 66 |
| Hector Santiago | 69 |
| Bob Amick | 71 |
| Nick Oltarsh | 75 |
| The Dark Side: When Things Go Wrong | 78 |
| Customers | 81 |
| Family | 89 |
|    Patrick Murphy | 92 |
|    Kevin Murphy | 93 |
|    Katherine Murphy | 93 |

Final Thoughts                94

Recipes                       95

   Brunch & Lunch            97

   Soups and Salads          113

   Appetizers                125

   Main Courses              137

   Sides                     156

   Desserts                  160

Acknowledgements              170

Index                         172

# About Murphy's

Located in Atlanta's trendy Virginia-Highland, Murphy's is the long-standing hub of neighborhood camaraderie and the choice destination for visitors seeking the epicenter of the district's shopping and nightlife. Tom Murphy's acclaimed restaurant brings in the crowds with the perfect combination of upscale comfort food, unpretentious service, a cozy, high-energy setting, and excellent value.

Chef Nick Oltarsh hails from Manhattan's Eleven Madison Park and Gramercy Tavern. His contemporary American menus reinvent what a classic should taste like — updated, simplified, made with fresh, seasonal ingredients from local markets. The Dutch Pastry Chef, Jon Hamstra, brings European artisanship to American dessert favorites while adding his own delightful new creations.

The interior combines rustic, exposed brick and French café doors with modern design elements for a light, airy effect by day and a warm, sparkling atmosphere by night. A new renovation added a sophisticated martini and

wine bar and sleek retail wine shop that showcases an extensive and user-friendly wine collection, plus hosts weekly wine tastings and seminars. Murphy's has been awarded the Wine Spectator Award of Excellence.

In 2005 Murphy's also won the prestigious DiRoNA award, which is presented by The Distinguished Restaurants of North America to promote the finest restaurants in North America, Canada, and Mexico. It has been named one of the city's best restaurants by *Atlanta* magazine, voted best brunch and one of the top 50 Atlanta restaurants by *Jezebel* magazine and has also been featured in *Bon Appetit* and *Gourmet* magazines.

*Murphy's chef, Nick Oltarsh, and I take a rare moment to relax on the patio at Murphy's. Enjoying a fine bottle of wine and a good conversation is one of my pleasures in life, but one I didn't have a lot of time for the first 25 years of owning Murphy's!*

For 25 years I've been welcoming people into Murphy's restaurant. After such a long time, now seemed like a good time to share the story of how we came to be one of Atlanta's favorite restaurants.

I wanted this book to be a lot of things: a way to pass the story of Murphy's down to my children and grandchildren, a recognition of all the talented people who helped make Murphy's a success, and a guide for potential restaurant owners. I also wanted it to be entertaining — the kind of book you can sit down and enjoy with a glass of wine — just like a good Murphy's meal.

A lot of people think, "I can cook, so I can open a restaurant." If you're one of those people, please read this book first. Not that I want to discourage you, but as you'll find, owning and running a restaurant is about a whole lot more than food. I'd love for you to learn from the lessons I've learned the hard way.

We ran into so many roadblocks along the way that sometimes I can't believe we made it to where we are today. But I'm a big believer in how the universe works. I've learned many lessons in my life, but the greatest lesson is that if you do God's work, remain humble, and have a passion you are committed to, you will succeed. I learned the roadblocks I found were really there to keep me from going in the wrong direction, or from going backwards. And that doors that seemed to be closing were just there so I would take another path. The right path.

We made a lot of mistakes along the way. But everything we did we approached with the same level of commitment. I believe that is the reason we ultimately succeeded.

You'll see some photos of me when I first opened Murphy's at the ripe old age of 21. Back then I wore a beret, which suited my self-image: a street-wise, scrappy kid who had a dream. I don't wear that beret now, but I still feel as if I'm chasing a dream (and like to feel I'm still young!). I've learned that after 25 years, you mellow into what you do best. For me, what I do best is owning Murphy's restaurant.

On these pages, I'll be sharing who I am with you. But this journey isn't just about me. It's about all the folks who helped make Murphy's a success. Along the way, many of the most talented chefs in Atlanta have wielded their magic in the Murphy's kitchen: Rob Atherholt, Lou Locricchio, Shaun Doty, Gerry Klaskala, Michael Tuohy, Alon Balshan, and Hector Santiago. You'll hear from all of these folks and many others who had a hand in the success of Murphy's restaurant. You'll also hear from friends, mentors, customers, and family members.

Thanks to every one of you.

— Tom Murphy

*"Murphy's is an extension of my kitchen. It feels so much like home that once I went up there wearing my slippers, and ate at the bar."*

— Catherine Lewis, long-time customer

When Tom Murphy opened his first restaurant, he called it Murphy's, More Than a Delicatessen. So we thought about calling this book *Murphy's, More Than a Cookbook*. We have plenty of delicious recipes in the book, including a few from some of Atlanta's best chefs. But this book is more than recipes. It is also the story of a journey. The journey of a little deli into an award-winning restaurant that has become an icon in Atlanta dining. It is also the story of the journey of a young boy who started in the food business by selling hot dogs out of a metal cart to pay for his schooling and became one of the most successful restaurant owners in the country.

He wouldn't say that or write that. But I can.

Murphy's was also called Murphy's Round the Corner, because of its location right down from the intersection of Virginia and North Highland avenues. After a move in the early 1990s, it is located at that intersection and serves as a landmark for the neighborhood. Now it is known to everyone simply as Murphy's and has generated a quarter of a century of memories and recipes, which we share in this book.

It is also full of lessons for anyone who aspires to open a restaurant. (Lesson #1: It's not just about the food.) Sometimes folks I spoke with were hesitant to talk about the times things didn't go well. Tom also wanted to share his knowledge and the lessons learned in his 35 years in the food business (I'm counting the hot dog stand too — he's not that old!) so I encouraged them to tell me about when things went less than smoothly. I think you'll enjoy hearing about what goes on behind those kitchen walls too.

Many industries are known for attracting people with big egos. The restaurant industry is one of them. Tom Murphy is not one of those people, as will become apparent when you read his story. He is a very modest man and is more comfortable giving credit to others for his success. But this book wouldn't be a true picture of Murphy's restaurant without hearing from other folks, with their thoughts about Murphy's and about Tom.

Murphy's is one of the most successful, beloved restaurants in Atlanta, with a "cult-like following" as the renowned chef Gerry Klaskala put it. Murphy's celebrates its 25th anniversary in 2005, and is unique both in its longevity in a city where restaurants come and go quicker than you can say pinot noir, and for its continued success.

From its beginnings as a glorified cheese shop in the basement of a funky building in a pre-gentrified neighborhood to its current, beautifully designed location just a few blocks away, Murphy's has grown up. And the neighborhood of Virginia-Highland has evolved with it. In fact, many folks give Tom Murphy credit for being one of the catalysts for turning it into one of the trendiest neighborhoods in Atlanta.

But despite all the changes, Murphy's has never lost its comfortable feel, where folks come to grab a glass of wine and a plate of calamari and relax at the beautiful curved granite bar. They come with their families to the most famous brunch in town on the weekends, if they can get in amidst the line of folks willing to endure lengthy waits for the famous biscuits and egg dishes. They come for elegant, yet casual dinners, prepared by Nick Oltarsh, one of the best chefs in town.

I've been going to Murphy's ever since it was in that funky little basement in Virginia-Highland and I do declare, there is no better brunch in town. But I was still surprised how people's eyes would just light up when I told them about this project. People are passionate about Murphy's restaurant. So if you want to know what the theme of this book is, I would say, "food and passion." Those are two of my favorite topics — how about you?

— Jan Butsch

# Murphy's Wine Shop: Vintage 1980 and 2005

*Functional rather than elegant may be the way to describe our first wine shop in our location on Los Angeles Avenue. Wasn't it clever the way we stored items in baskets on stools? And note the whimsical, yet economical decorative touch of the two empty honey bottles on either side of the lamp.*

*Look at our wine shop now! We have an extensive wine collection and we host wine tastings every Tuesday.*

# Beginnings: "Hey, You're the Cheese Man!"

It's hard to believe it's been 25 years since I started Murphy's. One night my wife Susan and I went to a movie. We were walking out of the theater holding hands, feeling like we were 21. Four people: a husband and wife, their daughter, and granddaughter, came over to us. The father pointed to his daughter and said, "We used to bring her to Murphy's when she was this size," pointing to his granddaughter. It was great to know that generations of people have eaten at Murphy's.

A lot of people recognize me now when I go out. It still gives me a bit of a thrill. The first time I was recognized for being in this industry was also an exciting experience, but in a slightly different way.

I was driving home late one night from The Cheese Shop we had in the Atlanta Municipal Market (where I worked after high school and also while I attended Georgia State University). Atlanta is a major metropolitan area and there are some areas that are a bit unnerving to drive through; you just don't want to linger. I came to a stoplight in one of these areas, and this huge guy in an old dilapidated Lincoln pulled up next to me. I nervously glanced sideways and saw he was pointing at me and gesturing wildly. It was, in fact, rather disturbing. It crossed my mind that his excitement was possibly drug-induced, and I thought about just gunning it and running the light, but my curiosity got the better of me. That, plus I was sure his big old Lincoln was more powerful than my beat-up Toyota Corolla, and I'm not much of one for high-speed chases.

So I cautiously rolled down my window and looked in his direction. Full of enthusiasm, he yelled, "Hey — you're the Cheese Man! I know you — you're the Cheese Man!" I just busted out laughing, partly from relief and partly because it just felt so good to have someone recognize me. It still does.

My career in the food industry started at a very young age, before I could even drive. And before I could even vote, I swore I'd never work in the restaurant industry. So how did I get here?

*This is a photo of me at the opening party for Murphy's on December 1, 1980, lifting the first of many toasts to friends and family in my very own restaurant. A friend gave me the mouse because of my nickname as The Cheese Man.*

# "A Loaf of Bread,
# A Pound of Meat,
# All the Mustard
# You Can Eat!"

Visitors to Peachtree Battle Shopping Center in Atlanta in the late sixties may recognize that slogan. When I was 11, that is what I would yell out from my hot dog stand (a metal cart) to passersby as I sold hot dogs.

It wasn't my first entrepreneurial effort. My dad, Joe Murphy, was an attorney for the Coca-Cola Company, so when I was 10 I figured I could help out the neighborhood ladies and make a few dollars by carrying crates of 24 bottles of Coke. But the bottles were way too heavy, and the customers weren't lining up for my service, so I quickly abandoned the effort. I guess that was my first lesson in giving customers what they want.

When I was in 6th grade, my dad bought a hot dog stand for my brother and me. My parents had moved to Atlanta from New York so my dad could work for Coke. This was a real New York hot dog stand, a novelty in the sleepy town that Atlanta was at the time. My dad would go to Redfern, the manufacturer of the hot dogs for The Varsity, and buy their irregular-sized hot dogs. So you never really knew what size you were going to get — they might be a little beanie weenie or they might be a foot-long.

I'd push that cart all the way to Peachtree Battle Shopping Center and sell those hot dogs. People seemed to love to see a young kid hustling so much. Of course, I had to eat a few hot dogs each day. My record was 12 in one day.

*"I paid about $400 for that hot dog stand. It was one of the best investments I ever made. It wasn't really legal for my sons to be selling, but because they were so young, no one ever bothered them."*

In the fall we would take the cart down to the Woodruff Arts Center and sell hot dogs to people going to the symphony. On weekends my dad and I would take the cart down to the Coca-Cola building on North Avenue and sell hot dogs before Georgia Tech games. One day we even met Robert Woodruff, the chairman of Coke and the man credited with making it the most famous brand in the world.

Once I also met J. Paul Austin, who was the CEO of Coke. I was rolling the cart out of a parking garage as Mr. Austin was walking to get into his car, a yellow Jaguar. He looked at me and joked, "That's the way The Varsity started." Right as he was speaking to me, the umbrella on my stand hit a light fixture on the ceiling of the garage, which fell down, ripping out part of the light fixture. He didn't say anything about that.

I learned a lot about being in business from the hot dog stand. I loved the experience because people thought I was *something*. It gave me a lot of confidence.

*I spent a lot of time with this hot dog stand, selling hot dogs and eating a few myself every day. After I opened Murphy's, we used it for catering events for the opening of Old Navy stores. My son Patrick also used it to sell hot dogs at our neighborhood pool during the summers. He ate his share of hot dogs out of it too.*

# I'll *Never* Go Into the Restaurant Business

I come from a family where everyone worked, so it never occurred to me not to work. We were New Yorkers. My grandmother lived on East 82nd and worked at B. Altman for more than 40 years. She worked well into her 70s because they didn't know how old she was.

My mom, Alice Murphy was a nurse at Piedmont Hospital and worked the 11:00 p.m. to 7:00 a.m. shift. We had six kids in our family. There was always something going on at my house on East Wesley Road.

I had Attention Deficit Disorder when I was young, but that was back before they really knew what it was. I just knew I didn't seem to catch on to things as quickly as other people. Mom was pretty progressive and she knew I didn't quite fit into the normal form of education. She got me extra tutoring and gave me lots of love, which gave me the confidence to believe in myself, even when I wasn't doing so hot in school. Ironically, being ADD has contributed to my success as a restaurant owner. You definitely need to be able to multi-task. That's one lesson I'd like to share: Today's disability may be tomorrow's success story.

When I was in eighth grade, my dad left Coke. I was at Christ the King School, but there was no money to pay for my school, so I worked and paid my own way. My mom moved to New York to finish her degree at Columbia; she became the private nurse for Sunny von Bulow and worked for her for years. In Mom's later years she got cancer and moved back to Atlanta. We lost her in September 2001. I am very grateful I

was fortunate enough to be able to spend time with her and take care of her during her last years.

Another reason I had to earn money at a young age was to pay for a little childhood mischief: When I was in third grade, I was hanging out with some friends and they decided it would be fun to put sugar in our teacher's gas tank. Well, it ruined the engine and cost $600 to fix. My dad made me mow lawns to pay for it.

When I was 15, I lied and said I was 16 and got a job at McDonald's on Peachtree Street. I would go in at 11:30, just when they were getting ready for lunch. I'd get all worked up before I went in because I knew it would be really busy. I worked in the kitchen, as a bun man and at the fry station. I liked the energy at McDonald's, but I couldn't handle the fast pace when the lunch crowd hit.

## John Huey, Editorial Director of Time Inc, New York:

*"I grew up next door to the Murphy family. They were an exotic family, to say the least. Dad ran a cheese business out of the backyard and did a lot of ministering to the poor. Mom was a nurse, and there were lots and lots of kids.*

*Tom, or Tommy, as we knew him, was always my favorite because of that personality he still has today. My most vivid memory of him is as a young child, standing down by the curb of East Wesley Road, selling hot dogs from a little stand he had cobbled together. As you might expect, they were good. And they sold. So maybe Murphy's is really a lot older than 25."*

In ninth grade I had a friend who was the head busboy at Brennan's. It was a franchise of the famous New Orleans restaurant located on West Paces Ferry Road, and was best known for its jazz brunches. (Though I don't think we called it brunch back then.) One of their most famous dishes was a flaming Bananas Foster.

I went to work there for the first time on a Friday night and was introduced to a whole new world. There were crazy waiters, gay waiters, drunken kitchen chefs, and an old guy in the dish room who knocked back any leftover drinks. It was a madhouse and I went home exhausted after each shift.

One Sunday after I'd been there about six months, we were setting up tables for Sunday Jazz Brunch. My manager, Iggy, told me to bus only one table at a time that day. Well, I thought I knew better than he did, and I did two tables at once. After he told me for the third time to do only one table, I flipped my wrist mockingly and said, "Okay, Iggy." To which he replied, "You're fired."

Now I know he was right. I may have been bussing tables faster, but doing that you slam one waiter with two new tables at the same time. I learned then that I didn't always have the whole picture, and maybe other people might have something to teach me. That was the only time I ever got fired, but I was actually relieved. The work was exhausting and it wasn't really the best lifestyle for me at that young age. I was in high school at St. Pius, but I was always too tired to participate in any sports.

My first experience with catering came from the same friend who got me the job at Brennan's. It was a party for Coca-Cola Bottling and I worked from 7:00 a.m. on a Saturday to 1:00 a.m. on Sunday. I made $100 and was so exhausted I couldn't

*We had six kids in our family so there was always action at the Murphy house. Maybe my chaotic upbringing helped me cope with the stress of the restaurant business. From the left, this is me, my sister Ann Marie Pendley, my brother Chris and my dad, Joe at our St. Patrick's Day dinner in 2005.*

go to school on Monday. I couldn't understand why anyone would want to do this.

After Brennan's and the catering experience, I swore I would never go into the restaurant business. The work was too hard, I thought, and the people were crazy.

# The High School Bleus

But I wasn't out of the food business for long. My dad's friend, Russ McCall, had a wine and cheese shop at Lenox Square and I started working there the fall after my sophomore year. I had helped out in previous years during the holidays, doing tasks like rolling cheese balls, etc., so I was eating bries and Danish bleus from the time I was in middle school.

I'd go to parties in high school and all the other kids would bring pretzels and Miller beer. I'd bring boursin cheese on apples, strawberries, and wine. I was something of a duck out of water, and didn't really belong in high school. I was younger than most of my classmates and wasn't into football. Instead of talking about touchdowns and field goals, I was learning about Bordeaux and cheese. I was also still struggling with my schoolwork, and sometimes felt like I was dumb. Looking back on those days, I tell my kids, "I wasn't much of an academic. I was a student of life."

I went to work for Russ McCall and by the time I was a senior became the assistant manager. I gradually grew to love the gourmet food business because I became knowledgeable about it and people respected my opinion. That made me feel important in a way school never did. Granted, that was back in the days when knowing what havarti was put you on another level. We're talking about the Velveeta Era, and the selection of cheese in Atlanta didn't go much beyond American. So I was educating the north side of Atlanta about how good Jarlsberg and Gruyere were. This was also the heyday of Blue Nun and Lancer's. I wasn't quite old enough to drink wine, so I'd say, "I'm told these wines are very good."

Then the era of the gourmet grocery hit Atlanta, with stores like Halpern's and Carmine's opening. But as soon as one of these stores tried something, the grocery stores would do it (and do it cheaper) so a gourmet grocery store really couldn't succeed.

Working in that cheese shop made me feel good about myself. And there is something else I've held onto from those days at the cheese shop: my wife.

*Susan, my wife, and me in the early days.*

Susan Lawler is from Virginia, but had moved to Atlanta to go to fashion college. She was working at The Tennis Lady, a shop upstairs from my wine and cheese shop. One day, her friend sent Susan down to the shop to check me out. She must have liked what she saw because she said she had tickets to see Mitzi Gaynor and asked if I would like to go. We dated from then on.

Elizabeth Terry, owner/chef of the critically acclaimed restaurant Elizabeth on 37th in Savannah, worked at the cheese shop. That was the first time I worked with a talented chef, but I didn't know it then.

# Market By Day, School By Night

*I like to think we introduced many Atlantans to the concept of fine cheeses. We had 34 types, imported and domestic. I loved giving people samples of cheeses and seeing them enjoy a type they had never heard of before. Back then Velveeta was the height of elegance.*

My dad opened a cheese shop in Macon and another one in downtown Atlanta, in the Municipal Market with a partner who unexpectedly died. So the summer after I graduated high school I helped my dad run the shop at the Municipal Market. The Market, on Edgewood Avenue, had been established in 1923 and was modeled after city markets in Europe where customers could buy fresh produce from small vendors. There were about 30 vendors there and it was a little like the country in the city: you could buy rabbit, seafood, and soul food, such as chitlin's, ham hocks, and pigs' feet. Ours was the only cheese purveyor.

The market was almost shut down in the early seventies by the Atlanta Health Department because some of the vendors — not us, of course! — had trouble meeting health standards.

But then it was renovated.

To this day, Susan calls Murphy's restaurant "The Shop" because of those days at the Municipal Market.

I went to college at Georgia State. I ran the market shop in the day and went to school at night. I got a lot of business from school because professors would write lunch orders on the board for the next day's delivery.

A group of Grady Hospital doctors ate at the market every day. They often asked my opinion on their food selections, and I felt like I had an identity and a position of respect. We all want to be fulfilled and appreciated, and once you find that it doesn't matter what you are doing. Finally, I felt that it was okay to be different — felt I was a part of something real and valuable. That's what the cheese shop gave me.

We realized fairly soon we didn't make a lot of money just selling cheese, so we added sandwiches, and then business really took off. Soon we became more of a sandwich shop.

Our deli combo was $1.50; soft drinks were 20 and 30 cents; a pound of potato salad was 99 cents; and cheesecake was 89 cents. We offered more than 34 types of cheese, imported and domestic, at a time when American Kraft Singles was the cheese of choice for most shoppers.

At the end of my junior year at Georgia State, I took a management class and my professor was Dorothy Brawley. She assigned us the project of doing a feasibility study on opening a business. My project was on opening a neighborhood deli. At that time Silver Palate and Balducci's were popular restaurants. My concept was kind of a combination of Carnegie Deli and Silver Palate. I wanted to marry the concept of a sophisticated New York deli with the friendliness and comfort of a small-town

*Some of my early marketing materials: card (on left) and sandwich on roof (below)*

Southern store. I was born in New York and my family was from the North. My parents were both Yankees and my dad had taught me about the concept of a New York deli. I had fond memories of those delis and thought the South needed its own interpretation of the deli concept.

Dorothy loved my idea and actually went to the bank with me to get financing. She really helped me make my dreams come true. Suddenly I had a plan and I had the knowledge. Now all I needed was money.

I sold the cheese shop for $15,000 and borrowed $10,000. I was only 21 and couldn't get investors. So I opened the first location for $25,000. The name wasn't difficult to decide. In New York, the delis are known by the family's name. So Murphy's it was.

When I worked for Russ at his cheese shop he used to tell me, "Tom, if you just focused on one of your business ideas, you could do really well." I'll never forget those words. Being successful was so important to me, and it's been a driving force all my life.

When I got ready to open my first location, Russ was closing all his wine and cheese shops. He told me he would sell everything from one of his shops for $5,000. So I went to Lenox Square on a Friday night and took it all: furniture, fixtures, light bulbs, and even a toilet bowl. That was the beginning of Murphy's.

*I still remember how exciting it was to have my photo in the newspaper.*

Virginia-Highland is one of Atlanta's most popular neighborhoods for shopping, dining, and nightlife. The neighborhood's name derives from the intersection of Virginia and North Highland avenues, and its history can be traced back to the 1800s when the first farmers settled in the area.

After the Atlanta Street Railway Company opened up the Virginia-Highland area to suburban development in 1890, developers began buying farms in the area and subdividing them for residential and commercial uses. Houses, streets and businesses were developed close to the trolley stops.

Atkins Park was one of the first areas developed in the early 1900s, with bungalow homes lining the streets of St. Augustine, St. Charles and St. Louis avenues.

Businesses quickly followed the residential growth. Although there were a few small commercial establishments near the intersection of Virginia and North Highland avenues in 1908, most of the development began in 1925. Atkin's Park Restaurant opened in 1927 and is reported to have the oldest liquor license in the City of Atlanta.

A stable neighborhood for decades, the neighborhood

began to decline in the 1960s and many middle class families left for the suburbs. Single-family homes were converted to apartments and property values decreased.

In the early 1970s a few families began moving in and property values again rose. The Virginia-Highland Civic Association was formed in 1975, with a mission to fight a proposed interstate through the neighborhood. After a long and costly battle, the freeway was stopped. Commercial revitalization followed about a decade later. Atkins Park Restaurant was renovated and commercial real estate developers and real estate investors bought up other commercial properties in Virginia-Highland. Exterior renovation work was done on the buildings, as well as parking improvements behind them.

Today Virginia-Highland is one of Atlanta's most desirable neighborhoods. The neighborhood's historic structures, which include the Samuel M. Inman School, the 1904 Adair Mansion, and Fire Station #19, as well as historic homes, give the community a distinct sense of place.

*History excerpt courtesy of the Virginia-Highland Civic Association*

*The famous late photographer 'Panorama Ray' Herbert shot this photo of the intersection of Virginia and North Highland avenues at the Murphy's St. Patrick's Day party on March 16 in 1985. While 'Panorama Ray' scrolled his camera from left to right, I ran to get in the photo twice. See if you can find me!*

# A Neighborhood Waiting to Happen

I had the idea of the neighborhood deli. I had a business plan and the capital to make it happen. Now I needed to find the neighborhood. I found what I wanted in Virginia-Highland. My dad knew Linda and John Capozolli, who owned the popular Capo's Restaurant in Virginia-Highland. They really were pioneers for the neighborhood, which had become run down in recent decades. When they opened Capo's in the late seventies, it was seen as something of a gamble. But John was attracted to the area by the sidewalks. He said he saw a neighborhood waiting to happen.

The Capozollis also owned a building at 1019 Los Angeles Avenue. I was bidding on the location against Steve Gorin, the founder of Gorin's Ice Cream. I won out and set about making a deli out of it. Steve and I became friends and watched one another as we both journeyed through the food industry.

The shop was in the basement of a house and I did all the construction myself, even knocking out walls. Family and friends I enlisted spent four days just jack hammering. My manager from the cheese shop, Elaine Matchett, came along. Then, at a bakery, I found a fabulous cook named Julie Clifford. I needed her because I knew nothing about cooking. The three of us opened Murphy's.

My late father-in-law, Beverley Lawler, who we all called Bear, owned a large advertising agency in Norfolk, Virginia and he designed our logo.

*We worked for days getting our location ready to open. It's a good thing I'm blessed with loyal family and friends who aren't afraid of hard, messy work.*

*It was such a thrill to see my name in lights! We called ourselves Murphy's Round the Corner because we were just down from the intersection of Virginia and North Highland avenues.*

### Susan Murphy:

"My dad was a very successful entrepreneur and Tom was a lot like him. My dad came to town and Tom took him to see the building on Los Angeles before he leased it. It housed an antique shop at that point. I'll never forget the look on Tom's face as he was sharing his vision of what Murphy's would be with my dad. He knew that was what he wanted to do. My dad just smiled as he listened to him."

# Closed on Opening Day

Our opening was scheduled for November 30, 1980. But a funny thing happened on the way to the opening. We had a fantastic pre-opening party, but got way too much into the spirit of things, if you know what I mean. We had to delay our opening by a day until everyone recovered. So we officially opened on December 1, 1980. I was 22 years old.

Then we hit another little snag. My brother-in-law had worked on the plumbing, but apparently he didn't quite finish the job. So on opening day, the pipes clogged up and water backed up. We had about an inch of water on the floor and it was streaming out the doors.

Now, I might have taken these mishaps as bad omens for my brand new business, but I didn't see it that way. You just wipe up the floor and move on. And people were showing up anyway and walking through water just to see the place. That's when I knew it was going to be successful. We had about 50 people show up on that first day and they were so enthusiastic, I just knew it would take off.

*We were exhausted from getting Murphy's ready to open, but that didn't stop us from having an opening party. Here are some of the first customers ever at Murphy's.*

# Creating a Sense of Belonging

And it did work out. Murphy's was built on the shoulders of earnest women who loved hospitality and cared about food. They gave their heart and soul to it, and the neighborhood responded. Julie was a wonderful chef and people loved her cooking. And Elaine was the workhorse behind me; she kept me organized.

As the neighborhood gourmet deli, we started creating relationships. One of my goals was to give people a sense of belonging. I wanted people to be able to eat there or take home components to make a sandwich, or take home a bagel or a piece of cheesecake.

Our sandwiches were $1.25 for a half, up to $2.25 for a hot Reuben. You could create your own sandwich too. That price was listed on the menu as "it depends." We had platters for $2.95 — a plate of three homemade salads was one of the most popular — and we had daily specials on sandwiches, soups, and entrees. We were the first restaurant in Atlanta to serve a sandwich on a croissant, which set a trend in the city.

Because we served fresh food, we got a reputation as a healthy restaurant. R. Thomas, owner of R. Thomas Deluxe Grille, which has been in business almost as long as Murphy's, called it a "sixties' natural restaurant, with hippies, fresh food, vegetarian chili, and great dishes aimed at eating right."

I wanted Murphy's to be a part of everyone's day every day. To me, the concept of a delicatessen meant the best the neighborhood had. This was a new concept for the South. Atlanta didn't really have a deli culture. Russ' shop was about the closest thing to it, and of course he had shut down. My goal then was the same as it is today: Sell a high-quality product at a good price in a comfortable atmosphere.

Of course the meaning of "comfortable" today in our present location is a little different than it was back then. We could only seat about 20 people in the dining area, which had brick walls painted white. Sometimes people would buy food to take out, and go outside and sit on the steps. Open shelves held

glassware, bottles of wine, and Lucite canisters of coffee beans.

When we first opened, we didn't have a license for wine and beer. It took us a while to get one because we were close to a church.

I had my office in a room upstairs with a lounge chair in it, where I often slept at night. I started work at 6 a.m. for breakfast and worked until midnight. I did that six days a week for five years. Back then I had that type of energy. I was driven and the business was growing.

We had all kinds of people who wanted to help. An elderly lady who lived across the street wandered over one day and asked if she could work for us. Her name was Zelda Wiggins. She was built like a spark plug and was just a burst of energy. She said, "I have nothing to do, Can I be your host?" We said, "Sure!" Then she asked if she could make biscuits for us, which she did every Sunday morning. Zelda worked with us for a couple of years and when she wasn't working, she would keep an eye on the place after we closed up for the night.

Another woman who contributed to my success was Katherine Huffaker — a huge influence on me. A really eccentric Christian Scientist, she walked around the neighborhood delivering fruit and copies of the Christian Science Monitor to the elderly from a buggy. She tutored me when I was young, then lent me money and did the books for Murphy's in the early

*Early to-go menu. I was so busy I lost track of the years. We opened in 1980 but it just felt like it had been since 1979!*

days. She loved the journey of learning and seemed to always have the right answer for everything. She really helped show me the right way.

The first time I saw Katherine I was in sixth grade and she scared me to death — she had a face like an old Indian woman, all weathered. She was in her 60's and thought heat was bad for you so she'd leave her windows open in the dead of winter, even when the drinking water for her cats would freeze.

For a while before we were married Susan lived in an apartment behind Katherine's house. She told Susan that if I was going into the restaurant business, she needed not to worry about jealousy. (More on *that* later.)

Years later Katherine got ill and called me. I went to her house and she was in a lot of pain. I flew with her in my arms to Des Moines so her son could take care of her. She died shortly after that.

Her son sold her house and the lady who bought it knew we had been friends. She called me and said, "Tom, my husband and I keep hearing things, like something's moving around. We went up to the attic and found a box with a picture of her inside."

They gave me the picture and never heard the noise again. That, to me, was just more proof of Katherine's strong spiritual presence. I feel blessed to have had a lot of eccentrics like her in my life.

# Elaine Matchett:

"Tom and I were in the same management class at Georgia State. I had just moved to Atlanta and saw an ad for a job at the cheese shop on a board near where I lived. I walked into the cheese shop and Tom hired me on the spot. I had never done that type of work before, but I learned as I went along. My major was in management, but I started at the bottom at the cheese shop! I made sandwiches and sold cheese. Then when he opened Murphy's, I moved there with Tom. We worked together for about 10 years.

For me, there were two really special things about Murphy's. It was very personal: When guests came we would get their name and eventually we knew a lot of the customers by name. The other thing was the excellent food. I always told Tom that if I didn't work there I would still come there to eat. In the restaurant business you work a lot. But Tom always said, 'We work hard but we play hard too.'

*Elaine Matchett and Susan, two of the women who contributed to the success of Murphy's.*

At first he was hiring a lot of pretty girls. Finally I said, 'You have to find the ones who will actually do the job, not just look pretty.'

We laughed a lot and had a lot of fun. Of course we had our share of mishaps. Once when Tom was on vacation it seemed like everything went wrong. We had a fire in the meter box and a cash register shut down. Murphy's Law was in effect.

Tom is a really hard worker and a tremendous boss. He became like a brother to me. He really cares about the people who work for him and is an exceptional human being with great business sense."

## Julie Clifford:

"I was working at a bakery when I met Tom. He came in to look at all the breads. When we started I was the food person and Tom was the money person. We started small, with simple soups and salads and it just evolved from there. Murphy's was like a little kid with its own personality.

And we were the new kid in town, so we were busy fairly quickly. We became a part of people's everyday routines. For breakfast we had the Southern Crescent: a croissant with ham and cheese. People would come by every day for that. They had their favorites and would get pretty irate if we ran out.

We were all over the place with our food. We made it all from scratch and had a good range of different foods. Vegetarians could find a good selection; our veggie chili was a big hit.

Zelda Wiggins was about 4 ½ feet tall and 75 years old. She loved to help us out and would carry a huge frying pan of eggs up the stairs to the kitchen to put in the warmer.

We worked some incredible hours and were closed only on Tuesdays, when we would clean up. People would still come knock on the door on Tuesdays, wanting to come in for lunch.

I left, went to Seattle and then came back and helped start the bakery, which was upstairs with the catering department. I had also seen some new things in Seattle and we added things like basil pesto bread. I worked there the first three years, and then after that I was there off and on. In fact, I got kind of burned out. In management, you're accountable when things don't go right. It can be wonderful, but it can also be really stressful. Now I'm a physical therapist assistant.

Tom was always very generous and gave other folks a lot of credit. He was quick to acknowledge people's talents. We had such great support from the neighborhood and Murphy's was really a catalyst for making it such a trendy area."

*Julie creating some of her delicious dishes.*

# Early Press and Customer Feedback

We started to attract the attention of the media. An article came out in the Intown Extra section of the *Atlanta Journal-Constitution* a month after we opened and said, "Murphy's is already well on its way to becoming a popular intown place." The writer, Donna Williams, referred to our tiny dining room as "reminiscent of the renovated basement of a home–simple, but cozy." She gave our food a glowing review and noted our extensive selection of gourmet products.

We got more reviews in local publications and business just kept growing. Just as I had hoped, we became a part of people's lives and a large part of my clientele from the Market followed me to Virginia-Highland.

*Back then people didn't really know what Virginia-Highland was so they said we were in Midtown. I didn't care as long as people came in and ate our food!*

Owner Tom Murphy calls his small restaurant, Murphy's 'Round the Corner, "more than a delicatessen." (Photo-Ray West)

## Murphy Opens New Deli In Midtown

### By DONNA WILLIAMS
Reporter, Intown EXTRA

We almost got lost when looking for Murphy's 'Round the Corner.

But we found it, and later decided we were happy we made it to the new Virginia-Highland delicatessen.

Murphy's 'Round the Corner is a small storefront-type delicatessen located at 1019 Los Angeles Ave. near the intersection of Virginia and North Highland Aves.

Its 23-year-old owner, Tom Murphy, calls his place "more than a delicatessen," and we couldn't have agreed more.

Open just a little more than a month now, Murphy's is already well on its way to becoming a popular intown place.

We had dinner at Murphy's. Instead of taking our food out, as most of the delicatessen's customers do, we walked up a few stairs to a tiny dining area.

The area was reminiscent of the renovated basement of a home - simple, but cozy. There were bottles of wine and honey on a mantle on one side of the room.

On the other side, there was an antique piece of furniture with plastic silverware and other necessary items. Part of the wall looked like a huge wine rack stuffed with all types of wares - many unfamiliar to us.

While waiting for our meals to arrive, we entertained ourselves by discussing the foodstuffs on the nearby shelves - things like sea salt, Irish oatmeal and "cocktail fishes."

Our food arrived after a short wait. The hot Reuben sandwich at $2.25 was delicious with a better-than-average amount of corned beef and Swiss cheese.

Murphy's Po' Boy sandwich at $1.50 was an inexpensive meal in itself. The sandwich was packed with a variety of meats, cheese, lettuce and tomato.

The big hit, however, was the quiche-of-the-day, which was ham and squash. None of us are long...

the quiche. The salad, composed of non-skinned potatoes seasoned perfectly and served on a bed of lettuce, was also a treat.

For dessert, we had chocolate cake, which was chocked full of black walnuts and pecans. One member of our group gave the cake, which is baked by a local bakery, the "supreme compliment" saying it "tastes good with a cigarette."

We also tried Murphy's chicken salad - one of the delicatessen's most popular items, as a store customer proclaimed. You couldn't have asked for a more meaty salad, but some it could have used a little more seasoning.

Some of the other popular items at Murphy's are its cognac and truffle, French and country pates selling from $2.99, Italian and other sausages, more than 50 varieties of imported cheeses (and access to 50 other types), "corner platters" and soups-of-the-day, which are offered on a rotating basis.

Lasagna and other pasta dishes are usually available for take-home and heat-up use.

Although Murphy's is fairly small in size, the delicatessen has a comparatively extensive selection of gourmet food items.

There are also plenty of natural beverages and several types of imported coffees which sell for $5.25 a pound or 50 cents per cup.

Murphy's is open from 8 a.m. (serving French pastries in the morning) until 9 p.m.

For those who have always wanted to take their lunch to work but never can find time to prepare it, Murphy's offers what we thought to be a unique service. You can call the night before and they will have your lunch packed and ready to take with you in the morning.

The delicatessen also caters for gatherings of up to several hundred people and will prepare gift packages.

Some customers may remember owner Murphy from the Municipal Market, where he ran a shop called "Murphy's The Cheese Man." His sister now runs the shop, which Murphy operated for five years.

Murphy, who is working on a marketing degree from Georgia State University, said he decided to open a delicatessen because he "lives in the (Virginia-Highland) neighborhood and felt there would be a need for a specialty food store in the neighborhood."

He said the sh...

*The Booth family, at left, lined up along with other customers for brunch on Sunday. They came every Sunday for years. Their daughter, Olivia, learned to eat lox and bagels at Murphy's.*

*A shot of our outdoor seating. People came and sat there for hours. I loved that they felt at home enough to stay.*

*A shot of our indoor seating. It got pretty crazy when the restaurant was full.*

## Some of the comments our customers made about our first location

"When I moved to Virginia-Highland in 1991, Murphy's was still located on Los Angeles Avenue across from the fire station, and I was just down the street. One evening, my parents and adult siblings came to pick me up for dinner before a Braves playoff game (still a novelty at the time). We walked around the neighborhood looking at the options and eventually made our way to Murphy's. My parents were studying the menu posted on the window when they were accosted by a friendly guy who seemed to be hanging out in front of the restaurant. 'Murphy's is really good,' he said. 'I'm sure you'll enjoy yourselves. If everything isn't terrific, Tom Murphy will make it right or give you your money back. And I should know; I'm Tom Murphy.' Needless to say, we entered and had a great meal."

*Jeff Alperin*

"One of my favorite memories of Murphy's was when it was around the corner in that little house. My mom and I would wait outside, sometimes for an hour, for that unbelievable stuffed waffle. We were always honored when Tom would stop by to check on us, as if we were royalty. Everybody recognized us, and even though times have changed and people have come and gone, Murphy's still feels comfortable and welcoming."

*Angie Wehunt*

"I remember eating at the original location, before it moved to the corner of Highland and Virginia. It was a very warm, comfortable place with an incredible atmosphere. I loved the outdoor seating area and the fact that all the neighborhood cats hung around looking for scraps."

*Mitch Leff*

"Back when Murphy's was operating out of the little place on Los Angeles, there were signs posted around to 'please bus your own table.' After lunch there one day, my husband carted his trash off to the garbage can, and I stood at the table and carefully swept all the crumbs, paper bits, and salt grains off the table into my plastic sandwich basket (former Girl Scout). As soon as I finished, Tom (whom I hadn't noticed before) approached me and thanked me heartily for busing my table so well ... and treated me to lunch that day!"

### Leigh Douglas

"I moved to Atlanta in 1984 from Providence, where I was working for the *Providence Journal*. I had been hired as the national feature writer for the *Atlanta Constitution*, and upon moving here was anxious to make myself feel at home. For me, one way to do this is to find the restaurant or café or bar in which you feel immediately at ease when you enter. In Providence, this was a joint called Leo's. In Tucson, it was the Shanty. In Atlanta, I found Murphy's.

I can't recall how I first 'discovered' it. At the time, I was renting a wonderful apartment in Druid Hills, but it had no laundry facilities. There was, then, a grungy (and that would be putting it politely) laundromat in Virginia-Highland, across the street from Highland Hardware. And most likely, while waiting for my clothes to dry, I ambled outside and into Murphy's (it was then on Los Angeles). I was home.

From that point on, if I was in town, I was at Murphy's either every Saturday or Sunday morning, or both, newspaper in one hand, coffee in the other. The wait staff knew that I wanted to get through my first two cups of coffee

*Here I am as the cocky kid in the beret, happy at owning my own restaurant.*

before I ordered breakfast, which took me through the A and B sections of the paper. And then breakfast, and then more coffee. On Sunday, with a 700-page newspaper in front of me, this could be a three-hour process.

I'd get there when the doors opened, but you couldn't help but notice that by 9 a.m. or so, there would be a wait. And there I was, leisurely strolling through Dixie Living, Sports, and Arts & Entertainment, while waiting customers cooled their heels. On some of these mornings I would chat with Tom and one time I mentioned my concern that I was hogging a table, thus preventing him from 'turning the tables.' He said—and I've remembered this always—that he felt his café should be like those in Paris, that once you occupied a table, it was yours for as long as you sat there, it didn't matter whether it was just you, coffee, and cream, or a party of five. The ultimate host.

I was never made to feel rushed, never once given even a subtle suggestion from the waiter. I felt at home.

While I enjoy the present location, my heart goes out to the old one, to that marvelous patio, that intimate feel. In later years, my wife (who lived in Paris for six years) and I would go to France and I saw for myself what Tom referred to. A table is yours 'til you decide it isn't.'"

### Rob Levin

# Mixing Family and Business

I never believed in partnering with or hiring family members. In a crunch, I let the rules slide, however. I knew I could call on my sisters when I was desperate and they would respond to my brotherly begging and pleading.

I once had a catering chef who left right before we had a weekend job to pull off. My sister, Alice Whaley, pitched in and saved me on that one. After a bookkeeper left, my sister, Ann Marie, came to help out.

At that point we were growing quickly and bookkeeping was crucial. Lots of guests assume that if you are busy you are making a fortune. The average independent restaurant nets 6%. You work on $.06 on the dollar so every penny needs to be accounted for. You don't lose your money typically in just one place but it's a death of a thousand needles.

Ann Marie came in to help me stabilize the bookkeeping situation and wound up staying for more than five years. I know she got at least one thing out of her experience at Murphy's. Once morning I sent her across the street to the bank to get change for the restaurant. She came back with the change – and a date with the branch manager. Ann Marie and Chip Pendley eventually married and I lost my bookkeeper but gained a banker. My sister was a huge support then and still helps me out in a pinch.

Now let's talk about Susan.

Despite my ridiculous hours at "The Shop," as she called it, Susan and I were still dating. I'll never forget the first time I met her father. We had gone up to Virginia to see her family. He was out in the backyard and I wandered out there to meet him. I thought he was the gardener! After I introduced myself, he said, "What are your intentions toward my daughter?" "No good," I said. Lucky for me he laughed.

*Susan and I are smiling here, but there were a lot of times when we worked together when we weren't. We decided it was best if we didn't work together – a decision we've never regretted.*

Susan had helped me out at the Market and now at Murphy's. But we didn't always see eye to eye. With Murphy's becoming more successful, I was starting to attract the attention of some of the ladies in the neighborhood. There was one in particular, Donna, who used to come visit. One night during the first summer we opened, we were closing the restaurant and Susan was there wiping off a table. We heard a knock on the door and Susan said tiredly, "Please don't open it. We're closed."

I saw it was Donna, wearing a pair of white hot pants, so naturally I let her in. Susan couldn't believe I had opened the door. She was so mad she just about wiped the stainless steel finish right off the table. Donna floated in and picked up a pound of coffee, then went to pay Susan, who walked over to the register, seething. The money practically levitated in the air, it was so thick with tension. I opened the door to let Donna out and she stopped and gave me a big old kiss. Right on the lips. Of course, I smiled at that and dreamily watched her walk away, wanting to catch every last glimpse of those cute little hot pants.

I turned back toward Susan, who glared at me and then lifted that dirty towel and heaved it across the room with the superhuman strength normally found in women only when their children are trapped under a car (or when they perceive themselves to be wronged by a man). If we could bottle that energy, we wouldn't need power plants.

Anyway, that towel smacked me right in the middle of the forehead, sending my beret flying and practically knocking me down. "You clean this $%#@* place yourself!" she yelled, and stomped away.

A few months later Susan gave a customer change and it fell in her coffee. The woman said it was okay, but I thought she should have given her a new cup of coffee. So we had a difference of opinion over that one.

The last straw happened shortly after that. We had these long deli cases where we kept the salads. I was getting some salad out for a customer when another customer walked in. Susan was helping that customer, so she flung open the door to the deli case, while my head was still in it. The door slammed into my head and I'm stuck in the case. I was stunned, and waited for her to apologize and help me out. Instead she started laughing. Then two customers who are watching are laughing so hard I think they are going to wet their pants right there in my restaurant. I'm the boss and everyone is laughing at me.

So I fired her. But then I married her. She was the only girl I knew who would come to see me at the Municipal Market. I wanted to marry her because she accepted me for who I was.

Susan's family always had a traditional Christmas, so I flew up to Virginia as a surprise and proposed in front of her whole family. They loved it. Fortunately she said yes. We were married on August 28, 1982 and I took a whole month off for our wedding and honeymoon in Napa Valley and Lake Tahoe.

We bought our first home on Amsterdam Avenue from one of our customers. We bartered having our floors done with another customer, who did the floors in exchange for eating at the restaurant. I think he ate lunch there every day for a year.

---

Susan:

"We had been dating for five years. I was helping him with the shop as much as I could. I was also helping him do work on his house. Finally I put my foot down and said, 'You know, I'm helping you do all this work, and I really don't want to be making this big investment of my time and energy just so another woman can come along and benefit from it.' Sometimes it helps to be direct.

We did not work together well. We're both Irish and we're both headstrong. I wanted to help him out and wanted to work with him so I could see him, because he worked all the time. But we realized it was not a good idea. After we got married, I got a job in a doctor's office for awhile, then went to work for a travel agency. I tell people it's best not to have your family working in the business. I think it can destroy a family. I was always supportive of his career, but thought it was best if I went my own way. I grew up in a family where my dad taught us to separate business from family and he never had any of us work for him.

One thing Tom learned from my family is that you have to take time off. Tom has always worked so hard, it was tough for him to relax. My family rented a place at Nag's Head, North Carolina every year for one or two weeks. When we were dating, we invited Tom along. One year Tom didn't come and I met someone else and started dating him. Tom didn't miss the trip after that. My dad worked really hard, but he knew how to have fun. I think that opened Tom's eyes.

Shortly after he opened the restaurant I put some money in a savings account and took a class at Emory called 'Europe on a Budget.' I made Tom take three and a half weeks off and Elaine ran the shop. We spent a week in London, went to Scotland, then Paris, and took a bike trip through Burgundy. I believe that trip really opened up the world for him; he could see what was out there. He realized that you must have balance. This business can be really hard on families and it would really be difficult if we both had full-time careers."

# A Bit o' the Green

With a name like Murphy and a big Irish Catholic family like mine, throwing a St. Patrick's Day party was a given. I always thought St. Patrick's Day in Atlanta was kind of boring, so I decided to start my own party. We closed off Los Angeles Avenue and had a block party with Irish music, dancing, food, and beer. We always served corned beef and cabbage. The party grew each year, and then it became our busiest day of the year. We added a 5-kilometer road race, a Gael of the Year award, and a Trip-Around-The-Block sweepstakes. I'd get other local merchants to chip in prizes, so customers could win breakfast at Murphy's, wine at The Corner Wine Bar, dinner at Capo's, and dessert at The Dessert Place. We'd have hot dogs and ice cream for the children and a Best Dressed Irish Kid contest. It was a great party.

On our 10th anniversary, we went all out and rented a huge tent. The night before, it poured rain and the tent had two inches of water in it. But we got tons of pine straw and laid it down in the tent and people came anyway. They were dancing in the mud.

When we moved to the current location, we had to stop having the parties. The liability issue was a major concern. We still celebrate with a nice dinner each year and my daughter's Celtic dance troupe performs.

## Murphy's 4th Annual St. Patrick's Day Block Party And 1st Annual Roadrace.

The festivities include Irish food, traditional Irish music and Irish dance. Gael of the year award. The "Win a trip around the block" sweepstakes, and the 1st annual children's sweepstakes. There's something for the whole family.

The block party and roadrace is sponsored by Murphy's, Coors Beer Co., and Virginia Highland Business Association and Civic Association.

### Sat. March 16th
2 to 10pm (Roadrace is at 9am)

The block party and roadrace is located in wonderful Virginia Highlands

*How can you be Irish and have a restaurant named Murphy's without having a great St. Patrick's Day party? In the photo below are my brother Chris, my dad and me at one of our St. Patrick's Day parties. The other two photos show some of the amazing entertainers we had each year.*

# From a Deli to a Restaurant: The First Coffee Mug

Our deli business was going along fine for the first few years. Then we started the evolution into a restaurant. I can tell you exactly at what point that happened: We were selling all of our food items in baskets and our coffee in Styrofoam cups. Then one day my dad came in. He had always supported me in my business ventures, from buying me the hot dog cart to setting me up as the Cheese Man. Now he was a regular at Murphy's, and that day he was carrying his own coffee mug.

"You serve great food, but everything is in Styrofoam," he said. "Your coffee tastes terrible in these cups."

So I bought real coffee mugs to please my dad. Just that small move shifted us, and people perceived us as offering higher quality. And they were willing to pay an extra quarter for the coffee.

But switching to real coffee mugs meant I had to buy a dishwasher and hire people to bus the tables. Then we needed to add silverware and slowly our evolution into a restaurant began. All from that first coffee mug.

## Joe Murphy:

"When Tom first opened, Murphy's was like a replica of The Cheese Shop. He didn't have a chef and he was serving coffee in styrofoam cups, just like McDonald's. I told him that if he was going to become what he wanted to become, he needed to go more upscale. That was the spark he needed to make him think. I've told him a lot of things over the years and I never know what he'll listen to. But he listened to that.

Tom's forté is his ability to recognize his own limitations. Whether he needed the skills of a cook, a chef, or an accountant, Tom would go out and find the expertise he needed for the benefit of the restaurant. He was always a couple of steps ahead of where he needed to be.

Every three years, he made changes to Murphy's. He added a patio, or table service, or a new cook. His was the first restaurant in that area to serve brunches. That was back before the area became the yuppie capital of Atlanta.

The tables were so small there, and there was no privacy, but it had a flavor to it that the yuppies loved. If somebody proposed in that location, everyone knew it."

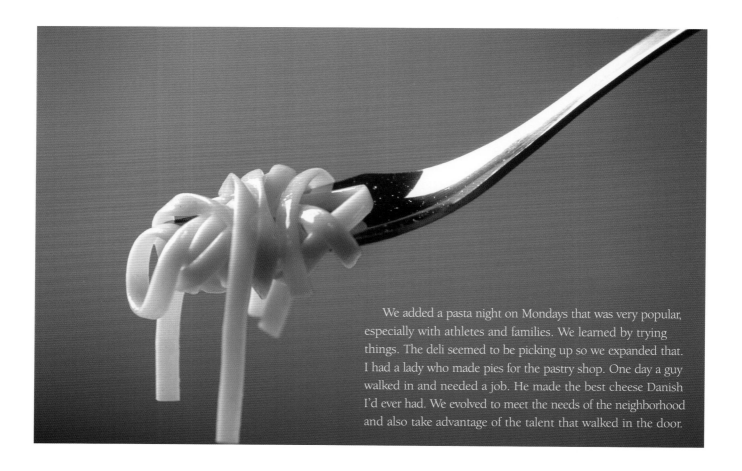

We added a pasta night on Mondays that was very popular, especially with athletes and families. We learned by trying things. The deli seemed to be picking up so we expanded that. I had a lady who made pies for the pastry shop. One day a guy walked in and needed a job. He made the best cheese Danish I'd ever had. We evolved to meet the needs of the neighborhood and also take advantage of the talent that walked in the door.

# Hiring Talent

From the very beginning I knew I needed lots of talented people to help me run this restaurant. I've been extremely lucky with finding amazing people to take me where I wanted to go. Four of those folks were food consultant Mike Hufler; my long-time general manager Ed Thomas; my accountant Bob Wagner; and Shelley Pederson, who came in to run catering for me. Following are their stories of those days at Murphy's. You'll also get a lesson in the catering business and learn why I will never, ever do catering again.

Mike Hufler was a customer and a friend of mine. We shared meals and I realized that in addition to being a food consultant for Houston's, he had a great palate. Because he worked for a national chain, he was able to bring me flavors and ideas from around the country that weren't being done in Atlanta. At that time I didn't have a chef, only kitchen managers. So Mike gave us creative and unique recipes and our kitchen managers would implement them, which is how it works in big chains.

## Mike Hufler:

"I am a food consultant and primarily work with chains, such as Houston's, Houlihan's, Rio Bravo, and Ted's Montana Grill. Murphy's was one of the few non-chain restaurants I ever worked with.

I met Tom through a mutual friend back in the late eighties and he mentioned that he could use some help, so I developed some soups and salads for him. The most popular item I developed for him was Murphy's Best Pasta.

Tom was just running a little operation back then. His facility was incredibly challenging to work in — the kitchen was in the basement and the dining floors were upstairs. He did a great job considering what he had to work with. And he always wanted to be doing something new and exciting.

I give Tom a lot of credit for what he has been able to do. He really is one of the reasons that Virginia-Highland is what is it today, and the new Murphy's is the center of the retail community."

## Ed Thomas:

"I worked with Tom Murphy for almost 12 years. I started in 1988 as the night manager and after three months became the general manager.

I had grown up in California and was working for TGI Friday's, which brought me to Atlanta. I was a trainer and traveled to new locations. I thought then that there was no way I'd stay in the restaurant business, so I moved to the hotel business for 3 1/2 years. But my managers at the hotel told me I needed more food and beverage experience to advance my career; that's how I started to work with Tom (in what I thought would be a temporary capacity.)

But I stayed. I loved the fact that it was a neighborhood restaurant.

I had a lot of restaurant and management experience, which is, I think, what Tom saw in me. Tom was the people person and I was the numbers guy. I handled all the accounting and the money, although there wasn't a lot of money to count back then.

One thing that attracted me to Murphy's was that it was not a chain. We had the ability to change things if we didn't like the way it was, which was one reason for our success. If something was broke, you could fix it. We could make changes to the menu any time we wanted. Tom had very high standards and if something didn't measure up, he

*We loved this mural and thought it really captured the spirit of our restaurant. We thought the 3-D table over the air conditioner was a particularly creative touch.*

would just say, 'You are not serving that tonight.' With a chain, you got whatever they cooked and it went out.

We were really busy, and it was grueling. We were serving breakfast, lunch, and dinner and it was not unusual to have waits of 90 minutes on the weekends.

I didn't believe I had the passion for the restaurant business, but spending time with Tom helped me develop that. He gave me the free will to run the restaurant the way I wanted. Sometimes we would butt heads in a big way. We might scream and yell in the back room, but

when we walked out the door we walked out with one mind. We shared the same goals and vision.

The partnership worked because we operated with mutual respect. It was a hard decision for me to leave Murphy's because it had been so much a part of my life. But I moved to Charlotte, North Carolina and bought a restaurant there, an Italian family-style pizza and pasta place called Avanti. There were a lot of good things and a few bad things that happened at Murphy's. The most important was that I enjoyed it all."

## Bob Wagner:

"I met Tom when he was The Cheese Man. My brother had an office in Grady Hospital and he would walk across the street to get a sandwich. He always ordered the same thing and was impressed that Tom always remembered.

I started visiting also, and we developed a friendship in the seventies. When I met Susan, I knew she was the right one for him. Before I married my wife, Elizabeth, I introduced her to Tom and Susan to get their approval. They approved and catered our wedding in 1985, even serving the champagne and Belgian waffles themselves.

My kids grew up in Murphy's restaurant. After our second child was born, I would take my first daughter, Laura, there every Sunday and we'd chat over Belgian waffles and whipped cream.

I had been working for a big accounting firm but decided to hang out my own shingle in 1990. Tom needed help with accounting, and said, "I don't do business with friends, but in this case I'll make an exception. Will you give me a hand?"

Talk about a leap of faith! I didn't know anything about the restaurant business. Now my firm handles close to 100 restaurants and I speak nationally on restaurant accounting. Tom was our first account and because he had faith in us, the other restaurant owners trusted us too.

I teach a class at Le Cordon Bleu College of Culinary Arts and I always start the class with these questions (and answers): How do you make a million dollars in the restaurant business? Start with two million. How do you make a small fortune owning a restaurant? Start with a large one.

The Buddhists say the only thing that's certain is change. This certainly applies to the restaurant industry. You have to change to survive. Either you're changing or you're dying. Tom has changed enormously over this 25-year period, and I applaud his efforts to change. That's not to say it was always profitable, and when he started the chicken delivery business I was certainly scratching my head over the idea of driving cooked chickens all over town, a short-lived sideline for Murphy's.

One change that took a while to happen was his decision to serve alcohol. For years he served beer and wine, and made mimosas and margaritas with wine. Every restaurant in the neighborhood had a liquor license except Tom. He was concerned about maintaining the family image of his restaurant. He finally got a liquor license and his revenue shot up.

Restaurant owners always have to be concerned about the "veto vote." If you have a car with four people going out to dinner, you don't want one person to have a reason not to go somewhere, so you've got to have a wide enough selection that all four people can find something appealing.

Tom and I talked several times over the years about opening another restaurant. It's hard to say what would have happened if he did. But I think the risk would have been too great and I'm delighted that he didn't.

When I ask my students at Cordon Bleu why they got involved in the restaurant business, many of them say they do it to make other people happy. To me the key to this business is service and passion. Tom Murphy has those two concepts as the guiding light in his life. To that, add his good business sense and you've got a successful restaurateur."

*Bob Wagner is a CPA with his own firm, Robert Wagner and Company, LLC*

## Shelley Pederson:

"I was born and raised in Milwaukee and happily living there in 1988, when a consultant hired by Tom approached me about working at Murphy's. I told him I had no desire to go there. 'It's hot down there,' I said. 'It's a free trip to Atlanta,' he said. 'Tom Murphy is a really nice guy and he has a great restaurant with just the right amount of Beemers and Mercedes out front. You could be a perfect fit there.'

I flew down and interviewed with Tom. He took me to Michael Tuohy's restaurant, Chef's Café. He was so wonderful and Virginia-Highland was so similar to the neighborhoods in Milwaukee. And Murphy's looked just like a gourmet market where I used to work, housed in an older brick building built in the thirties or forties.

Ten days later, I gave notice at my job.

Back in those days the catering part of Murphy's was box lunches and deli platters, and Tom saw that he needed somebody to take it to another level. I had worked for two gourmet markets doing off-premise catering but had never worked in a restaurant. I had to get used to using items off the restaurant menu for catering. My favorite was the recipe for Murphy's pasta. It is just sensational. I used to eat it about three times a week back then.

But catering is not just about the food. It's a lot about logistics — plumbing, electricity, and safety laws. To be successful in catering you have to know all about the non-food things.

There is a certain mindset to catering. With a restaurant you can track trends and plan for your busier times. With catering it's really different and can be wildly unpredictable. You have to learn how to deal with the peaks and valleys in the business. You generally make most of your money in December.

We really built up the business and at one point I had five salespeople working for me. Sometimes I would talk with corporate clients and they would say, 'Murphy's? Isn't that the little restaurant my wife takes me to for brunch?'

We had a lot of challenges, rooted in the fact that we did so much out of such a small space. We sometimes had to share space with Alon, the pastry chef, and you

*We've always welcomed families to Murphy's. Pictured here are David and Angel Ats at the back table and at the front table from left to right, Matthew Harper, Jonathan Herman, Pam Allweiss and Sabrina Harper.*

can't put garlic mashed potatoes with pastry cream, or you end up with garlic pastry cream. I had to go outside of the building to get from my office to the restaurant. I used to joke that if this had been in Milwaukee, you wouldn't have seen me until spring because we would be stuck in snow.

One of our largest events was the grand opening for The Container Store at Piedmont Road and Peachtree Street. It was the first store the company had opened outside of their home state of Texas and they were nervous about branching out. We served 900 people and ended up winning a national award for best food presentation (in January 1992, from *Special Events* magazine). We had been told to use their merchandise to serve the food, but to stay away from the kitchen area. So we did things like pass out hors d'oeuvres on clipboards and dust pans and used their bin systems for crudités and fruit. It was really a thrill when we won that award.

Catering is a wild business but it is very gratifying to put together a function for a great celebration in places that were not set up for food service. And we did have things go wrong. One Saturday in December we were just slammed with parties. There were events in

Alpharetta and Peachtree City and three in Midtown. We had an event for a corporate client in his home and had borrowed a van to transport the food. It was a horrible looking van and we looked like the Clampetts going to town. We were on the highway when all of a sudden blue smoke started pouring out of the van. We somehow made it to the gas station and called Tom. He and Ed Thomas came to get us and transferred all the food to Tom's car. We were an hour late to the set-up and that day I thought my life was flashing before my eyes. But on the other hand, I realized, it's just a party. No one is going to die.

Weddings are a challenge because you only get one chance to do it right. If someone has a problem with a meal in a restaurant you can give him a coupon or a free dessert or something. Not so with a wedding. It's like a Broadway opening.

We once catered a wedding with 100 guests at the Golden Key National Honor Society. The bride arrived two hours late. The father of the bride wasn't there because he had been arrested the night before for disorderly conduct after the rehearsal dinner. Well, the bridesmaids started in on the food before the wedding. I called Tom and said, 'There's a lot of women in fire engine red satin gowns eating all the food, Tom! You have to send more food!' He rushed more food down there.

We once did a seated dinner for 400 people for the Nuclear Regulator Association at the Georgia Freight Depot. The guests were from all over and there were several Japanese people.

The menu was complicated, so it was quite busy. As the servers were bussing the tables from the soup course, the captain came running in and said, 'Shelley, we are going to run short of soup spoons. All the Japanese ladies are wiping off the spoons and putting them in their purses. What do we say?'

The answer is you say nothing. Half our spoons were gone and we had no idea why they wanted to take rented silver flatware.

We'd had to hire outside staff because it was such a large event, but we thought we were working with professional banquet servers. As another course was being cleared, another captain came running in and says, 'You will have to fire some people.'

I said, 'What are you talking about?' He said, 'See those three guys over there? When they clear the wine glasses they are drinking all the leftover wine.' So now I have drunk guys serving, and I had to find someone to get rid of them.

Now everyone is waiting for sorbet course. We had put it in freezers, but they had blown a fuse and we didn't realize it. So all this wonderful sorbet that Alon had made was now ruined—it was totally liquid. I told Tom we had to do something because sorbet was listed on the menu. He made a quick run to Kroger, where he bought them

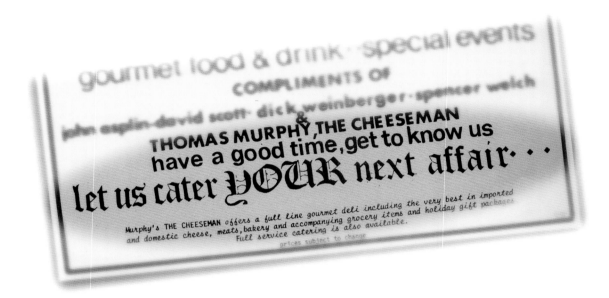

gourmet food & drink · special events

COMPLIMENTS OF

john koplin · david scott · dick weinberger · spencer welch

&

THOMAS MURPHY, THE CHEESEMAN

have a good time, get to know us

let us cater YOUR next affair...

Murphy's THE CHEESEMAN offers a full line gourmet deli including the very best in imported and domestic cheese, meats, bakery and accompanying grocery items and holiday gift packages. Full service catering is also available.

prices subject to change

out of lime sherbet, raced back and we scooped up lime sherbet for 400.

We had a lot of fun events as well. The old stainless steel hot dog cart that Tom used as a young boy was resurrected for Old Navy store openings. They wanted an all-American theme, so we served hot dogs, lemonade, pretzels, and brownies. They loved that we used the hot dog cart and hired us for all their store openings (until the last two or three when they stopped doing big openings). The folks at Old Navy *loved* Murphy's brownies.

For a few years we did a big brunch for all the Coca-Cola employees who ran the Peachtree Road Race on the 4th of July. I'd have to get up at 3:00 a.m. and we'd serve 700 sweaty runners.

Some of the folks who worked with me in those days were Doris Koplin, who developed recipes for Murphy's, and the late Desiree Marsh, a chef. Andre Crawford and Adam Vicinus were the glue that held it together and made sure vans got out on time.

It was actually very stressful, but Tom was always supportive and always on my side. For somebody who didn't like catering and didn't want to do it, he was really good with helping out. I worked with Tom until 1992 when he moved to the new location and decided to shut down the catering part of the business. Then I opened my own business, Beyond Cuisine Catering. I still go to Murphy's all the time, and use Murphy's and Alon's baked goods for my own company."

# My Big, Fat Catering Disasters

I used to carry a list in my wallet of the reasons why I will never go back to the catering business. Sometimes your mind can block out the negative part of an experience and then you are tempted to repeat it. I wanted to make sure that I never, ever let myself get back into catering. Restaurants and catering are both about food, but they are as different as night and day.

You'll find my list at the end of this chapter. Feel free to make your own copy.

At first I saw catering as another way of making Murphy's part of people's lives every day. I wanted it to be like the great delis of the world, like Carnegie's and Stage Deli in New York. Around 1982, people started asking us for delivery, so we started with sandwiches and salads. We soon got a reputation like Houston's: You always knew what you would get. Our food was good, tasty, a good value, and would be delivered on time. You never had to explain to your boss why lunch was late.

Then customers started asking us if we could do a hot lunch. So now the simple box lunch became more difficult. It doesn't take much staff to do a box lunch. But for hot lunches you need equipment and lighters. Now we were in the realm of a full-service caterer.

I would do anything in those days if it helped us pay the rent. I saw an opportunity because back then, there were only a few big caterers. Atlanta had Affairs to Remember and Proof of the Pudding. I saw it as an adventure. But I didn't know what I was getting into and did not know that business. So, as usual, I found people who did. I was constantly looking for people to teach me and to help. I have never had a problem opening my mouth to ask for help.

I went to a catering seminar and asked the leader who was the best caterer he had ever worked with. He told me he knew a lady in Milwaukee with a gourmet grocery, Shelley Pederson. So I called her and convinced her to come to Atlanta. I told her I had a great opportunity for her here, that I didn't know anything about catering and needed someone to run it.

The cornerstone of all businesses is people who have vision and people who have heart. Without the two you don't get anywhere. I had the vision and Shelley had the heart. She loved catering and it showed.

For me, the psychology of a restaurant is that I'm throwing a party and you are going to be entertained. You are coming into my environment and I get the glory if you have a good time.

In the catering business, if it's a success, the host wins. If it bombs the caterer is blamed. You make an event for somebody and then it's over and it's such a letdown. You won't see those people again. I always felt I was missing the purpose of the event — I didn't get to know them.

Good caterers love the creation. They like to paint the picture and move on. They love that energy and don't like the day-to-day, mundane chores of running a restaurant. They like the constant change and creativity. But I like building relationships.

With a restaurant you have more of a routine and can schedule your staff. With catering you could try to make a schedule and on Friday you might have one lunch scheduled for the following week. Then on Monday the phone starts ringing and you get more orders. It was really difficult to manage the staff while also running a restaurant. It made me nutty. With a restaurant you can control your own environment. With catering, it was always a new environment, and often one that was not set up for food service.

My restaurant chefs just hated it. It takes a different psyche to be a catering chef, so ultimately I had to hire separate chefs.

Sometimes people would say, "Oh you're that little deli in Virginia-Highland," and we couldn't break into the upper-end markets. But the irony is that we were so hungry to prove ourselves that we did a great job. It took a while, but we were recognized as a solid, high-end caterer.

Once we were doing a lunch for Emory Law School. We got a call from them asking where their lunch was. The mystery was quickly cleared up by a second call. It was the DeKalb police telling us that our lunch delivery person had run over

a garbage worker. He was okay but had the wind knocked out of him.

Another reason I don't like catering: One bad experience almost put me out of business. Permanently.

When workers at a large company (which shall remain nameless) went on strike, the managers were asked to cover their jobs. The company asked us to prepare breakfast, lunch, and dinner for 300 people every day during the strike. A guy I had met in Europe came to visit and I put him to work for 60 hours a week. He said, "No wonder Americans are so crazed."

Everything went perfectly for three weeks straight. As the strike was ending we had two meals left. On a Friday afternoon in June we were doing a barbecued chicken lunch for 500. The chicken came in but we didn't realize it had been sitting in the back of a truck for way too long, and had gone bad. So we cooked it up, took it to the location and when we lifted up the chafing tops we realized what had happened. I had 500 people waiting for lunch and a whole bunch of rotten chicken.

At this point we were all so exhausted that we were working beyond our limits. But there was no choice; we had to figure out what to serve all these people. We got on the phone and called every Po Folks around. Lunch was two hours late.

Even though we had been getting letters all week telling us how good the food was, the company then decided they were not going to pay any of our $45,000 bill for the three weeks because of that two hours. I was beyond stunned. I couldn't even believe they were going to screw me over like that.

In the end, we only got paid because my dad was good friends with their general counsel and made a call. Murphy's came close to going out of business over that one deal. From that ordeal, I learned that you're only as good as your last meal.

Another time we were doing a dinner for C&S Bank at an old southern mansion on West Paces Ferry Road, for 15 people at $200 a head. The kitchen had never been renovated. We

plugged in the convection oven and blew out all the fuses in the house. We had to cook the entire dinner with sternos, and serve dinner by candlelight.

Weddings were hell. We'd sit down with the client at the beginning and plan a nice event within their budget. The day of the wedding the guests would show up and the bride would start demanding more (but didn't want to pay more). They would ask for extra champagne but when it was time to settle the bill, they were gone.

In 1993 we had to move Murphy's. So I thought about whether I wanted to keep the catering portion. I realized I needed to get back to what I did best and where my passion was. And that was running the restaurant. I sold the catering portion of the business and Shelley went out and opened her own company.

# Why I Will Never Go Back Into Catering

1   There was no glory for me. I always felt like the hired hand. In my restaurant I felt like guests were coming into my home and there was mutual appreciation and respect. I did not get that same feeling with catering.

2   Scheduling was a nightmare. It was impossible to predict events too far out, so staffing was difficult. We often had to hire people from temporary agencies and they might not show up. And they had no loyalty to Murphy's.

3   There were too many unknown factors: elevators that didn't work, workers who crashed vans. The ability to improvise in those situations demanded more talent than I possess.

4   The business is feast or famine. It's dead in January and solidly booked in December.

5   When the economy got slow, everyone went into catering. There was more competition from small mom-and-pop operations, who might not be legal or certified by the health department but can undercut you on price. In the restaurant business, if you serve a good value, your business could get better when times are bad.

6   Transporting food is different than serving food in your own restaurant. The food quality can change from the time it leaves the restaurant and it is more prone to spoiling.

7   Catering requires a big investment in equipment. Larger competitors would throw in equipment rental for free because they already owned it. To compete, I had to buy china and other equipment. But then styles changed, the equipment broke down and I had to buy all new stuff.

8   Tracking down the money can be a problem. You have to make sure you get a deposit on the front end and make sure you can locate the person with the check at the event.

# The Murphy's Contest: It's in the Bag

*The ultimate take-out:*
*the Booths and their Murphy's bag in Bermuda*

Just for fun, we came up with a contest idea that ran from May to August every year. People would take a Murphy's bag with them on vacation, and whoever took a photo of themselves with the bag furthest away from Atlanta won $100. The most creative photo also won $100. Once, we had a photo from India with a snake coming out of the bag. A woman sent a photo of herself in a convertible, wearing the bag. A couple told us a story of going to the Corn Palace in Mitchell, Iowa. They were setting up their shot with the bag and another couple came up and said, 'We already took that shot, so don't bother.'

This photo is of J.B. and Rick Booth in Bermuda, in 1994.

# A Moving Experience: How I Got Gray Hair

You may think owning a restaurant is about serving food. I came to learn it's much, much more. It's also about real estate, leases, parking, neighbors, and sometimes even political campaigns.

After I'd been in business for about 10 years, I heard Linda Capozolli was planning to sell the building that housed Murphy's. Without going into painful details, the building was bought out from underneath me and I was given three years to move out.

That's when I started having problems with the neighborhood. That's when my hair turned gray.

I met Peter Hand, an architect, when he started coming into my restaurant in the early days. He lived on Virginia Avenue and was renovating apartments there, one of the first renovation projects in the neighborhood. Virginia-Highland had started a turnaround, but it was still in the early phases. In the mid seventies young professionals were moving in and fixing up the houses, then commercial renovations started in the late seventies.

Peter and I looked at several potential sites in the neighborhood. The storefronts were pretty much original from the twenties and thirties. Not much renovation had been done. We found the present location of Murphy's, which once housed 20th Century Antiques and Monterey Market, a convenience store.

When word of our potential move got out, some neighbors joined forces and tried to oppose the move. Some people had been concerned about any commercial enterprises in the neighborhood and I got caught up in that. Then somehow the moving of my restaurant became an issue in Mary Davis' campaign for Atlanta city council. Here's a tip to would-be restaurant owners: Never do anything that can be linked to a political election. It can be publicity you don't want.

*This photo of the corner of Virginia and North Highland avenues pre-Murphy's is courtesy of Mary Turnipseed. She is an architect with Peter H. Hand & Associates. Peter Hand did the original design of the new location.*

There was an NPU meeting at Morningside Presbyterian to discuss the move, and about 380 people showed up, many of them opposed to me opening in a new location. Murphy's restaurant was at the end of the agenda. One of the reasons I went into the restaurant business was to make people happy — going to that meeting and seeing all those folks opposed to me just about broke my heart.

Cy Timmons was a popular entertainer in town with his own club. His mother-in-law, who was about 70, was one of my customers. She stood up and said, "I am older than 85 percent of you. If y'all don't like it, move out of the neighborhood."

As property values were going up, parking became more of a problem and the neighborhood was worried about that. Certain folks started to see any commercial development as bad. Here's another tip: If you're thinking of moving a business into a neighborhood, take the temperature of the balance of residential to business. You'll get a lot more things accomplished if the neighbors support new businesses. Everyone is happier if you can work together.

I hope people realize now that it's partly because of the new businesses that moved into Virginia-Highland that it became the desirable neighborhood it is now (and why their homes have increased so much in value). How many times have you heard someone say about their home there, "It's so great because you can walk to stores and restaurants."?

### Susan:

"When we lost our lease and had to move I thought it would kill Tom. My dad tried to get us to leave Atlanta and move to Virginia, but Tom was determined to move the restaurant and stay in the neighborhood. We just

*Susan and me with our sons, Patrick on the left and Kevin on the right, where the patio is now.*

couldn't believe what was happening. Some of our close friends didn't show up to the zoning meetings because they couldn't believe we would have a problem. That move aged us about 10 years.

He was so worried about the move and how to recreate the same atmosphere and what the customers would think. Ed and I said, 'Tom, if you build it, they will come.'"

After our battles with the neighborhood were over, we had to work out all the details of opening the new location. My goal was to recreate the old place. I wanted it to be like your favorite piece of furniture — not new, but warm and comfortable. I thought only Peter Hand could do that. And he did.

### Peter Hand:

"After we decided on the new location, Tom and I would go over to the site in the evenings after Monterey Market was closed, drink a glass of wine and just watch the neighborhood, planning the new restaurant.

Our goal with the design for the new Murphy's was to cling to its roots but be a bigger version of itself.

We were trying to capture the architecture of the neighborhood and wanted to bring a residential scale into a commercial setting.

We wanted the space to feel intimate, like the kind of space where you would serve dinner in your own home. The seating capacity was 96, so we incorporated a lot of smaller areas to give it an intimate feel.

This concept also related to the quality of the food. Tom wanted to serve food that was elegantly prepared, similar to what you'd want to serve in your own house.

We also wanted an environment that would be attractive to the entire family. One of the reasons Murphy's was so popular in the original location was that couples with children came in often. It was a place for young families to gather.

The Chevron sign at the corner was huge back then, and we were concerned that the large amount of light would hurt the ambience of the restaurant, so we added the planting area in front as well as the canopies. We also built the walls in the restaurant tall enough so you wouldn't see the headlights of the cars.

The ceiling in the old location was green, so we painted the ceiling in the new location green.

Tom was really worried his customers would not feel comfortable in the new place. He is exceptionally interested in making sure people who come into Murphy's are pleased with the experience, and he is attuned to every small detail that could make the experience even better. We wanted to make Murphy's a delightful place, but not so trendy that it looked out-dated three years later. And we wanted the atmosphere to support the food.

I had to fight Tom on one idea. He wanted to do rotisserie chickens and have the oven up front. I said no to the chicken. 'You'll look like a Kroger,' I said.

The brick at the front of the restaurant is all original. We added a wine section with storage behind it, a white marble counter, and pastry cases. The move cost $100,000. The restaurant was closed for one week.

Two weeks after we opened, a guy came in and said, 'I like this place. I never liked the old one.'"

The first day we opened the new Murphy's I sat up front with a bottle of wine and watched all these dump trucks go down the street. Finally it dawned on me that they had torn down the old building where the first Murphy's was and I was watching the remains go by. It was really a kind of bittersweet moment. I was watching my past rumble down the street in the back of a pickup truck. I just sat there and kept drinking wine.

Now I realize having the building torn down was the best thing that could have happened. People can't go back and say, "This is where Murphy's used to be." The building is gone. Now it is a parking lot for Highland Hardware.

# Improving My Little Sandwich Shop

Today I'm a restaurant, but when I first opened I was a deli. They run on different economic models. When you open a restaurant, just a sandwich won't make it. You have to provide ambiance and entertainment and synchronize them so people enjoy the experience. You have to feed the mind and the heart. With a deli, you feed the heart and the body.

Another difference between a deli and a restaurant? About $10 a plate.

In a deli you work three times as hard to make the same amount of money.

When we moved to our new location the space was too large to focus on breakfast and lunch only, so I looked for new ideas and scoured trade journals. I invited chefs to come work for me and consult. (More on my amazing chefs on page 55). I also scouted through cookbooks, took ideas, and redeveloped them.

*I love this shot: three generations of Murphy's at our new location. There's my dad on the left, followed by Kevin, Patrick and me.*

Another reason I read trade journals is that restaurant owners often have big egos and they would spill the beans about what made them successful. I could look at what was happening in restaurants on a national scale and apply it locally.

How do you decide you have enough sandwiches and soups? To bring something new on meant you might hear from customers who loved old stuff. We were always value-sensitive. We wanted people to think they got more than they paid for — the wow factor. To raise prices a nickel meant sleepless nights for me.

If there was a consistent theme, it was that the more you changed the better you got. If you strive to keep yourself the same, you die. But the challenge was to keep your identity, and still continue to change.

I was constantly looking how to improve this little sandwich shop.

Another thing I always looked at was new trends in dining. Who would have thought years ago that people would pay money for a bottle of water?

For 19 years we served breakfast every weekday and brunch on the weekends. But then Americans' eating habits began to change. Starbucks and other coffee shops opened up and suddenly people stopped eating breakfast and would just grab a cup of coffee on the way to work.

But when you've done something for 18 years, you're hell-bent on not losing it. After the coffee shops opened, our breakfast business fell from $1000 a day to $650 a day over the course of a year. I increased my advertising and used coupons. I spent three years doing anything I could think of, trying to recapture the breakfast market. I finally threw in the towel and we gave up breakfast on weekdays, but our weekend brunch was still remarkably popular.

The Dessert Place had been a popular fixture in Virginia-Highland for about 20 years. They closed right around the time I quit serving breakfast. The day after we stopped serving breakfast, I made up the lost revenue in serving desserts and late-night coffees. I felt like I had angels looking out for me.

I thought, "Wow, I closed for breakfast and now I'm making more money! Maybe I should close for lunch and dinner too!"

Our take-out business was doing well — we did $4000 a week in that area. Again, Americans were changing their habits — cooking less, buying more takeout. We decided to start a chicken home-delivery service and I hired a guy to run it for me. Well, we found out that people love home-delivered hot chicken dinners, but they all wanted them at the same time and we could only do about eight an hour with the vans I had. If I had the staff and the vans, we could have sold 500 chickens between the hours of 6:00 and 8:00 p.m. So we closed that down.

Years later I got a phone call from a friend. "Your chicken guy is on 'America's Most Wanted!'" he exclaimed! I'm willing to bet my entire wine cellar I'm the only person in the world who has ever heard those words before. Apparently, my employee was a pedophile, a fact he conveniently left off of his job application. Fortunately he was caught and put away.

Then Whole Foods, Publix, Kroger, and Harry's in a Hurry opened and began to take the take-out business away from us. My sales dropped from $4000 a week to $2000. I again fought to keep that part of the business for a year but then gave it up. But then Indigo Restaurant, which had a side business called Indigo to Go, closed and I got back the business. Every time I made a move and focused on what I did best, I made money.

*Susan and me in our new location. You can't tell it because I'm wearing the hat, but going through that move is what made my hair turn gray!*

Shots of our new location before our last renovation. Our goal was to maintain the warmth and comfort of the previous location while upgrading the atmosphere to match the food.

53

# Tasting Trips

One of the best parts of owning a restaurant is eating in other people's restaurants, all around the country. Every vacation was a business event. We would go in a restaurant and I'd say, "I'm just going to go look in the kitchen." Everywhere I went I got to know the owner and the chef.

*Ed Thomas:*

"We were in New York, where we went once a year on a tasting trip. Out of the middle of nowhere, we ran into two people who knew Tom Murphy. One was a waitress who knew Tom six years ago.

I learned my lesson on the first tasting trip. In one 24-hour period we went to the top 10 to 12 restaurants in town to get ideas, taste things, and look at trends. With just two or three of us, we ordered 5 or 6 appetizers and 10 entrees. Well, there we were at the top restaurants in town with amazing food, so I ate it all. Not a good idea.

One of the best things about a career in the food industry: I've been lucky enough to eat at some of the best restaurants in the country."

# A Parade of Talent

As I've said, I never had any problem asking people for help. Unlike some restaurant owners, I am not a chef. I am a businessman. So I had to seek out cooking talent to make my restaurant what I wanted it to be.

Julie Clifford, my first chef, really made Murphy's. People just loved her cooking. After that, we had so many talented people come through the kitchen. I also often hired consultants, people I admired to help me out. I'd do anything to keep the wheels of creativity going.

It's been a real joy for me to see people who have worked in my kitchen go on to open their own successful restaurants. I feel like I've been a bridge to their success. When I look at this list of amazingly talented folks who have contributed to Murphy's, I feel so proud:

Lou Locricchio: Thumbs Up Diner
Rob Atherholt: Crescent Moon
Shaun Doty: MidCity Cuisine
Alon Balshan: Alon's
Gerry Klaskala: Aria
Michael Tuohy: Woodfire Grill
Hector Santiago: Pura Vida
Bob Amick: ONE. midtown kitchen, TWO. urban licks, piebar

Some folks may wonder why I'm including all these restaurant owners in my cookbook. Aren't they competition? Why am I telling you how wonderful they are and how great their restaurants are, and even giving you some of their recipes?

My feelings about competition have changed over the years. When I started out, and for many years, I was fearful of competition because I thought it was going to rob me. I thought if people saw me doing well, other businesses would copy me. But I learned that if you took care of what you had in your four walls every day, it didn't matter what opened across the street.

I've seen so many restaurants come and go in 25 years. Many were owned by people who were new to the industry, and didn't know what they were in for. I learned you build a business one customer at a time, but you can lose them 10 at a time. There were several good operators but they didn't have the right market.

I would see restaurants open for brunch and I knew they were coming after my business. They would learn fairly quickly that if you're open on Friday and Saturday nights you really don't want to open for brunch. It worked for us because we started out as a breakfast place and then moved to dinner, rather than the other way around.

Good leaders of industry are respectful of their competitors. They have the ability to communicate with them. It's just a lot more fun when you can both sit down and drink a beer together and share information. It's nice if a competitor can say, "There's a bad egg in the market — don't buy it."

Now, just like I've turned over my kitchen or my restaurant to these folks over the past 25 years, I'm turning over this chapter to them. You'll also find some recipes from some of these folks in the recipe section.

But one more word to all of these people: Thanks. Thanks for sharing your time, talent and friendship with me at Murphy's.

*Lou Locricchio started in the restaurant business when he was 12 years old, sweeping the floor of his dad's restaurant in Detroit. After earning a degree in restaurant and hotel management from Michigan State University, Lou worked for Houlihan's in California before coming to Atlanta in 1983. He opened the original Thumb's Up Diner in Decatur in 1984. After selling it to Rob Atherholt, he spent five years in the real estate development business. But soon he returned to his first love, and in 2000 opened a new Thumb's Up on Edgewood Avenue, adding a second location in East Point in 2005.*

Lou opened his first Thumb's Up in Decatur and various people kept telling me, "I love your new place in Decatur." I didn't know what they were talking about so I headed down there and saw that the menu was very similar to mine. So one day I asked Lou about it and he said he didn't know who the hell I was and that many of those recipes were his grandmother's. The worst part was, his food was much better than mine.

When I see somebody doing something good I make a friend out of him. So when I was getting a new chef, I talked Lou into selling Thumb's Up to my old chef, Rob Atherholt. Rob renamed it Crescent Moon. Then Lou bought property on Edgewood Avenue and opened a new location, which is where Jan and I met every week during the writing of this book.

If I choose you as my friend, you're my friend for life. When I saw Lou opening up, and saw how very talented he was, the best thing I could do was to extend the olive branch. Even though we were going to be competitors, we could still be friends.

What I am to the front of the house, Lou is to the back. Although we never worked in the same restaurant, we are kindred spirits. I always admired his "truth in food" — his is not pretentious and has all the flavors you might want. It almost has more polish than the environment it lives in.

Lou can be kind of rough sometimes, and I tease him that he has an old-man mentality, but he always puts love in his food and cooks like a young, wild Italian man, full of passion.

When I was working the high-volume brunch, I had two doors between the customers and me and it might be a few minutes before we picked the broken eggshells up off the floor. But Lou stood in front of his audience and cooked 200 to 300 brunches. He was a marvel to watch — like a machine. He still gets behind the line when he doesn't really need to, to keep his hands in.

## Lou Locricchio:

"I opened Thumb's Up Eatery in Decatur on Valentine's Day in 1984. This guy started showing up a few weeks after we opened and he would just sit at the bar, not really saying anything. We used to make fun of him. Then one day he told me he was Tom Murphy and he had a restaurant in Virginia-Highland and wondered why my recipes were so similar to his. I told him I lived in Dunwoody, worked in Decatur, had never heard of him or his restaurant, and didn't even know where Virginia-Highland was. He kept coming into the restaurant and we became really good friends, and have even shared staff. One of his breakfast cooks came to me to train, went back to him, then came back to me, and is now my general manager.

Back in those days Tom couldn't boil water and his biggest fear was not being in control of the kitchen, so he was always looking for talent for his kitchen. Most people in the restaurant business are kitchen people. Many are chefs who have been in the kitchen for years. Tom is a businessman. He became a pretty decent cook, however, and now his menu is pretty sophisticated. I don't think he ever got over his fear of the kitchen, though.

He's been smart enough to leave the cooking to his chefs and he always hired powerhouse chefs. He doesn't need to be back in that kitchen; he just needs to know what's good.

When I'd known Tom for less than a year I told him I needed some money for my business. I don't even remember what for. He said, 'Why don't you take a ride with me?' He took me to the bank and co-signed a loan for me.

I thought, nobody does that kind of thing. I was stunned, and said, 'What if I don't pay this back?' He said, 'That means I have to pay it.' I did manage to pay it off early, but I'll never forget what he did. Over the years if he needed something, I'd do it and he did the same for me.

We all say that Tom should be a politician. He can make friends with a dog on the sidewalk. I'm not that outgoing and spend 90 percent of my time in the back, but Tom is always up front shaking hands. He knows everyone and doesn't have an enemy in the world. Every-

*Lou Locricchio*

one who has ever dealt with him in the restaurant business will tell you that he is always there, always has a joke, and always has a smile.

Tom stays friends with his chefs even when they open their own places. He was the best man in Michael Tuohy's wedding. Alon made his name working at Murphy's, then left and opened up right down the street. Tom said, 'Competition is no big deal. It's all good. He's a great chef and will be a big success wherever he goes. I'd rather he stay in the neighborhood.'

When I opened my place on Edgewood Avenue, the first people through the door were Tom Murphy and his family."

## Alon Balshan, Alon's Bakery & Market

*In May 1992, owner Alon Balshan started Alon's Bakery with his father, Maurice. With just $500, credit cards, a loan on his car and some used equipment the two started their American dream. The small, 1,300 square-foot bakery offered three types of freshly baked breads.*

*In 1999, Alon opened What's The Scoop, a gourmet gelato shop, next door to the bakery and market.*

*Over the years, the store expanded in size and scope. Inspired by specialty markets in Europe and New York, Alon was passionate to bring a full-service gourmet market to Virginia-Highland. Ten years later in August, 2004, the bakery underwent a 1,000 square-foot expansion and allowed him to offer a full range of gourmet fare. The Bakery & Market now includes European-style pastries, cookies, artisan breads and wedding cakes as well as an artisan cheese selection with more than 80 varieties from local and global producers.*

*Since its opening, Alon's has become a neighborhood and city favorite, receiving high accolades from Gourmet Magazine, Atlanta Magazine, the Atlanta Journal Constitution and Creative Loafing.*

Alon Balshan

Alon Balshan came to Murphy's one day and applied for a job as a breakfast cook. I hired him as a favor to a friend, and because I just wanted to help him out. He is a massive man, about 6'7", so you can just imagine him in the basement kitchen of Murphy's. When he worked behind the line, he took up the whole line!

At that time I had a lady who made pies on site and we purchased desserts from other places. After he had been working there about 30 days, Alon came to me and asked if he could make some desserts. Why not? So he made a Napoleon and a cheese Danish that just blew me away. I realized Murphy's

needed to be making more than pies. Turns out I had one of the best pastry chefs in the city working for me, only he'd been back there cooking eggs for brunch!

Alon started making scones, Danish, and croissants and we eventually had a full bakery. He brought a European flair to Murphy's and we became known as a place to go for coffee and desserts.

He told me in Europe there are places that do only one thing, but they do it so well they have lines out the door, and in Israel there is a place that sells only croissants. At that time I was a deli, but was into catering and retail as well. Alon helped me figure out that when I moved, I really needed to focus on what I do best. Doing a few things great is better than doing a lot of things well. When I first moved to Virginia-Highland, no one was doing much of anything, so I felt free to start whatever I wanted. But suddenly there was a lot more competition and it was time to focus. I wanted to be a great restaurateur.

Alon is really passionate, and was always meant to open his own place. He left in December 1991 and opened Alon's in May 1992, right up the street from me! He moved into my neighborhood, so there was no getting away from him. It was a bit of a struggle at first because we turned into competitors, but we're destined to be friends for life.

### Alon Balshan:

"I went to work for Tom in July of 1988. I liked working with Tom and I could see the potential of Murphy's on the dessert side. It was a challenge for me to develop that area, and I did. By the time I left the dessert department had more than doubled. We made our own cookie dough, we made our croissants from scratch and we improved some of the other recipes.

I think that Tom and I had a special relationship and that's how we became the friends we are today. He respected my knowledge and me, and let me do most of what I wanted to do in my own department.

We went on a lot of tasting trips together. Tom is a 'no shame' kind of person. I learned from him the 'it doesn't hurt to ask' philosophy. Tom would go to the kitchen in every restaurant we went to, all over the country, talk to everyone and ask for recipes, or say, 'Will you come to Atlanta?' We always had a blast traveling together. We would eat three breakfasts, three lunches, and when dinner came we just had to stuff it down our throats."

## Rob Atherholt, Crescent Moon

*Rob Atherholt started in the restaurant business as a dishwasher and busboy at the age of 15 in his hometown of Virginia Beach, Virginia. By the time he was 19 he was sous chef at the Iron Gate House, an elegant, prix-fixe restaurant. Rob has an associate's degree in culinary arts and a bachelor's degree in food service from Johnson and Wales College. He was partner and chef of Coyote Café in Virginia Beach, and was executive chef of Taste Unlimited, a gourmet food and catering chain in Tidewater, Virginia, before moving to Atlanta to work at Murphy's, where he was executive chef. Rob is the founder, chef, and operator of Crescent Moon, a neighborhood diner with two locations in Atlanta.*

I met Rob Atherholt at a party in Norfolk, Virginia where my wife is from. He told me he was a part owner of Coyote Café. I had just eaten there the night before and thought it was a fabulous Southwestern restaurant so I told him if he ever wanted to come to Atlanta, I'd love to talk to him.

He called me a year later. I had heard he'd sold his interest in the restaurant and was a chef at a gourmet wine and cheese shop, which aligned so well with what we were doing with Murphy's and interested me even more.

Rob was a wonderful package deal because he came with his wife, Carolyn, who was a talented pastry chef. He was a hardworking chef, and he was instrumental in moving Murphy's from the old location to the new one. Without his tireless efforts and commitment to making it happen, we would not have been able to accomplish what we did. Rob was a critical part of making the new Murphy's open to a huge audience. He is good with food and also has a good organizational eye, so he helped us set up the new kitchen and save money.

I knew he wanted his own place. And at the same time my friend Lou was telling me he was burnt out, and wanted to get rid of his place. So I sent Rob to talk to Lou and they made a deal. Rob bought the original Thumb's Up from Lou.

### Rob Atherholt:

"I first met Tom Murphy in 1988. I owned a restaurant in Virginia Beach and his wife Susan's best friend lived across the street. They were visiting one time and I met Tom. He gave me his business card and said, 'If you ever want to leave here, call me.'

I had no intention of leaving. Ten months later I sold the restaurant and took a job as a chef for a gourmet catering and retail business, but I was getting tired of Virginia Beach. Then I remembered Tom and dug up his card. I called him up and ended up going to work for him in 1990 as the night chef.

Tom also hired my wife, who worked as Alon's assistant. But we never saw each other at work because she had to be there at 4:30 a.m. and I went in at 2:00 p.m. Plus, the bakery was upstairs and the kitchen was downstairs.

Tom gave me a lot of responsibility fairly quickly, and promoted me to executive chef. Ed was the general manager but Tom was always there to see what was going on. He was a very trusting and supportive boss.

I had never done breakfast before so that was new to me. We had a lot of breakfast recipes from Lou Locricchio and I updated the dinner menu, adding items such as Italian meatloaf and almond raspberry chicken. We updated the pastas and did a lot with dinner specials.

There were a few items I wasn't allowed to touch — like the basil chicken salad.

One big thing we did was standardize the recipes. They were all just typed on pieces of paper at that point. We got a software program that a friend of Ed Thomas' had developed and costed them out. It was a huge chore to get all the recipes entered and took an incredible amount of time. For example, we had to figure out how much a teaspoon of pepper cost. This hadn't ever really been done before and things like butter, salt, and pepper had not been figured into the cost of recipes; neither had the amount of waste you have in any restaurant.

The kitchen in the old location was very small, in the basement, so when you went from the dining room, you went through swinging doors and immediately down four steps. It was quite a challenge for the servers. The dishwasher was also in the same hallway where the servers came through. The walk-in was upstairs and outside.

We only had one flattop where we could cook potatoes and pancakes. So Tom had a portable flat griddle made that we could set on the char grill at breakfast time. That thing was huge and every day after breakfast, two people had to carry the 200-pound piece of hot steel up the stairs. Then at the end of the night, we had to drag it back down the stairs.

Inside we only had about 10 tables and more outside on the patio. We were always busy. At this point the

*Rob Atherholt*

restaurant was 10 years old and Murphy's had grown beyond being a neighborhood restaurant. People were driving from all over town to eat there.

After the move to the new location I stayed awhile and did the opening menu for the new location. We added the poached egg section for brunch.

We were closed for one week and after reopening in the new location, were immediately busy. The longtime customers came and new people found us because we were a lot more visible. But I'll tell you, there were some hair-pulling moments to get there. It took us a while to get it all together in the new place. Cooks would come and work a few hours, see how busy it was,

and they'd quit — never to return.

Our new walk-in was twice as big but it still wasn't big enough and keeping everything organized was a nightmare. And we found out that the kitchen designer did not take into account the crank handle on the kettle and everything was off by about four or five inches. Even the floor drains were off, and there was no way to move those. Tom was livid. We had to move the kettle, after all that time and effort spent designing the kitchen so you could just dump the water down the drain.

Staying on top of things was a real chore. We were so busy it was a whole new ballgame. We often hired folks from the Atlanta Recovery Center labor pool and I'd call them up to get three or four more sets of hands to help out. I'd sometimes have to enlist Tom's help. I remember going into his office and saying, "Tom, I need five gallons of diced tomatoes." He rolled up his sleeves, came out and got to chopping.

On the weekends we would still have customers waiting for brunch at 3:00 p.m. and it would take four of us making sandwiches and salads to get them out to the customers. Then we had to turn around and get ready for dinner.

We had lots of equipment problems. Ed and Tom bought a huge used steam table. It was so huge it had to be installed before the construction was finished. It was big and held a lot of food to keep it warm for service. But that thing broke down about three times a week. We'd have to get out the sterno and pans and run it like a great big chafing dish. This was particularly awful for brunch — cooking sausage and bacon and putting it in there. They would all get cold.

I was working 16 to 18 hours a day in the beginning. But we pulled through. I left after four years, in August 1994, and opened the first location of Crescent Moon in January 1995. We opened the Northlake location in May 2004.

After I left, Tom hired Gerry Klaskala as a consultant. That's when Murphy's transformed into what it is now."

## Gerry Klaskala, Aria

*Gerry Klaskala is the executive chef and managing partner at Aria, and also owns Canoe with partners George McKerrow, Jr. and Ron San Martin. He began cooking at 15 and entered a gourmet food show when he was 17, winning Best of Show. Gerry graduated from the Culinary Institute of America and was the chef and managing partner at Buckhead Diner. He also worked with the Hyatt Hotels Corporation for nearly ten years.*

*A recognized spokesperson for his industry, Gerry is frequently sought by local and national media outlets as an authority on American cuisine. He has appeared on NBC's "Today" show, "Live with Regis and Kathie Lee," and CNN, among others. During his*

*nearly 25 years of cooking, he has received numerous awards, including the 2001 Robert Mondavi Winery Culinary Award of Excellence. Gerry is often honored with invitations to represent Atlanta in culinary events across the country. He recently participated in the American Heart Association's Heart's Delight fundraiser in Washington D.C., and was selected to cook in the Great Chefs of the South event in Beaufort, North Carolina.*

*Gerry and Aria have been recognized in Bon Appetit, Gourmet, Food & Wine, Esquire magazine, and The New York Times. Opened in spring 2000, Aria serves contemporary American cuisine in a romantic setting.*

Gerry is my hero of heroes. He saved my butt. When I had to move the restaurant the old menu didn't match up to the new place. It matched the old location, with its funky interior, but my new place was much nicer. Rob took us from the old location to the new one, but he got burnt out. So I hired Gerry as a consultant to re-engineer the menu. Gerry came up with the brunch menu, which is now virtually the same as it was then. He brought it together for me. He taught me how great chefs think. Through him I learned that if you really trust people you can really grow. You have to trust or you will always be limited. I have so much more freedom now.

*Gerry Klaskala:*

"I met Tom through Bob Lynn, a vice president with Houston's. Of course, I knew about Murphy's. It is an institution, with a cult-like following. Tom is always looking to make his restaurant better and he reached

*Gerry Klaskala*

mount and Tom insisted on value, so it was like the three-legged chair of freshness, value, and quality. We put a hamburger on the menu. Tom wasn't sure that was part of who he is, but I thought he needed it because of the neighborhood feel of the place.

I'm now working with my 25th restaurant on creating menus. I know from consulting jobs I've done with other restaurants that you can create dishes that become iconic, the touchstones of your menu. The owner/operators may grow tired of them and are not sentimental about them. But for guests those are the memories. They want that particular dish. Guests will come back and say, 'What did you do to my dish?' They own the memory of it. It's like you are Mick Jagger and you have to sing 'Satisfaction' or Led Zeppelin and you always have to play 'Stairway to Heaven.'

There is one dish we created that is no longer there: The Big Murphy. It is a colossal baked potato vegged out — kind of a hippie thing.

When we put it on the menu, I told Tom, 'This is a great food item. Customers will love it. Your bottom line will love it. Every chef you bring in your restaurant will hate it.'

They hate it because it's a baked potato. Sometimes they were baked a little early and they weren't very pretty. And ambivalence is the killer of any dish. If you don't care about it, it dies.

out to me and told me what he wanted to do. I thought it was a great opportunity to help take a legendary restaurant to the next level.

Our goal was to move it from one decade to the next, get it into the nineties and position it for the next decade of culinary curiosity. Tom was a willing participant in the journey.

We put in four different menus — a new breakfast, lunch, dinner, and brunch. We left a few dishes intact but changed the majority of them. Freshness was para-

But ours was made with wonderful fresh vegetables and when it's done right, is a very soul-satisfying dish. I named it after Tom and also because in Ireland, potatoes are called Murphy. We had a full-blown discussion over The Big Murphy.

But my motto is food naturally tastes good, it only takes a cook to screw it up.

All of the menus were philosophically woven together. They had a common-sense approach and a certain wit about them. My tongue-in-cheekness with menus is subtle, sometimes not so subtle. There are lots of chefs who are wonderful in the kitchen but don't enjoy creating dishes. I love it — I just put on my Walt Disney hat and get to work.

The preparation took three months and then we implemented it all in one day. I remember the Sunday that we were putting in the last menu. We were beyond busy, getting crushed in the kitchen. It's not a big restaurant and I said to Tom, 'It cannot be this busy. You must have a dining room hidden with mirrors somewhere.' I have never seen a restaurant that size be that busy. I'd just left Buckhead Diner and was used to 7000 meals a week and here I was being getting pushed around by a little 110-seat restaurant.

The restaurant has maintained its sense of place in the neighborhood, its accessibility, and the menu still feels fresh. The food at Murphy's now is better than it has ever been. Nick Oltarsh, who I found for Tom, is a force to be reckoned with. I had a meal there recently and it blew me away. He is an immense culinary talent.

Tom has always reached out for talented people. The people who have contributed to Murphy's have been amazing — talent after talent after talent. You've had Bob Amick, Michael Tuohy, and Alon, who built his whole business over a mini model of a part of Murphy's. There has been a cavalcade of personalities and chefs and managers who have made Murphy's such a success. It has evolved and gotten better over time.

Some of the best coffee in the city is served at Murphy's. They have done a great job with their coffee program, that other restaurants would do well to emulate. And it's one of the quintessential brunch places in the city.

I love being around Tom. He's funny and very humble. We had a nickname for him: The Grinder. He has a lovely technique when you work with him — he just keeps grinding you. It's like going through a coffee mill. The reason that Murphy's is so successful is because of Tom Murphy. He is the classic entrepreneur and the kind of a guy who had a dream — and nothing was going to stop that dream. If you were deserving of a friend as good as Tom Murphy, you'd be doing really well."

## Shaun Doty, Table 1280

*Shaun Doty began his career at Restaurant Million in Charleston, South Carolina while attending Johnson & Wales University. Upon graduation, he relocated to Atlanta to work for two years under Chef Guenter Seeger at the Ritz-Carlton, Buckhead. Later, he pursued culinary stints throughout Europe, including time at fromageries, bread bakeries, and chocolatiers in France and Belgium, as well as working at the Michelin Three Star restaurant Comme Chez Soi. Returning to the United States, Shaun worked at Mirabelle in Beaver Creek, Colorado and then Savanna's in Southampton. He came back to Atlanta as the executive chef, and, later owner of Mumbo Jumbo, acclaimed for its seasonally influenced, modern American cuisine. While at Mumbo Jumbo, Shaun, a Slow Food member, frequently traveled through Europe, admiring the casually sophisticated cafés of Venice, Turin, and Paris.*

*Shaun's passion for brasserie cuisine and café culture led him to his next venture, MidCity Cuisine. The restaurant, which opened in 2003 and serves contemporary American brasserie fare, was recognized in Gourmet magazine as one of "America's Best Restaurants," in Atlanta magazine as "Best Outdoor Patio," and in Bon Appetit as "Best Casual" restaurant. In fall of 2005, Shaun became executive chef of the new Table 1280 Restaurant and Tapas Lounge at the Woodruff Arts Center.*

Shaun was a young, high-spirited man who was typically Irish in that he was gregarious and always happy. He had a quick step and a real sense of commitment to and passion for the food industry. Shaun was full of energy and ready to take on any job; he was always interested and curious. Even when he made a mistake, you knew he was sincere in his efforts to correct it, and I knew he was never just goofing off.

Shaun Doty

### Shaun Doty:

"I had just graduated from culinary school and was living in Virginia-Highland when I worked for Murphy's in 1991. Even at that time it had a super reputation. I wanted to make some extra money and Murphy's paid pretty well for help with catering.

I was young and inexperienced and kind of scared of Tom. It wasn't that he was intimidating, just that he was so successful. He was always there, on the job.

One time I crashed the catering van. Well, I just kind of bumped it into another car. I was scared to tell Tom. He was doing me a favor by giving me work and I didn't want to let him down. I thought, 'I am totally dead — I'll lose this gig.' I was really nervous telling him, and then he was so cool about it. Tom calmly listened to my story and said, 'Let's just keep going.' Having been in the business myself so long now, I know I'd be the same way, but it really made an impression on me at the time.

The restaurant was intimidating because it was so busy. It had a tiny kitchen with all this hustle and bustle. I was green and he was directing it all — like a traffic cop. I was overwhelmed by it all.

I've always admired him. I still look to him as an amazing restaurant operator and a wonderful mentor. He is intelligent, very sweet, and epitomizes the ideals of hospitality. Tom has a genuine desire to provide a comfortable dining experience. He created a unique ambiance that is casual, fun, and smart. But I know as an owner/operator that there is a lot going on to give Murphy's that appearance. The charisma of the owner is part of a restaurant's allure. He is very savvy in business and is modest in a very ego-driven industry.

He comes into MidCity Cuisine and gets all misty-eyed. 'I am so proud of you,' he says. It is so cute. I say, 'Stop, Tom, you're killing me.'

I've worked in Europe with big-shot chefs. Tom's up there with all the great ones I've known.

I am still very good friends with Alon, from the days working at Murphy's. What a coincidence — he is arguably the best pastry chef in Atlanta. Alon would give Tom a lot of credit for his own success. After working at Murphy's he could visualize what he wanted.

Since I worked there, Murphy's has matured. Tom has raised the bar, but still has the light, casual neighborhood vibe. He has trained new generations of chefs and raised the bar with that, too. The wine program is also very sophisticated. He is always pushing to do better. And I'm still a good client of Murphy's."

## Michael Tuohy, Woodfire Grill

Michael Tuohy's career began in San Francisco, under Chef Joyce Goldstein of Square One. In 1986, Michael moved to Atlanta to open Chefs' Café, which was selected as one of Atlanta's top five restaurants by Zagat, the Atlanta Journal-Constitution, and Atlanta magazine, and he was the force behind Chefs' Grill and the Ocean Club Restaurant & Bar. Michael has served on the local chapter board of the American Institute of Wine & Food, Atlanta's Table, Georgia Grown Co-op for the Organic Growers Association, High Museum Wine Auction, and he was co-founder of the Downtown Restaurant Association.

Michael partnered with Thomas Catherall in the acquisition of Indigo Coastal Grill, and was General Manager of Tom Tom Bistro. In 1999, Michael launched his own restaurant consulting service, which has included work for Murphy's, Coyote Café Cookbook, Francesca's in San Antonio, Fishmonger Seafood Grill, and Nashville's Sunset Grill, and Midtown Café. Michael and his staff have received acclaim from such publications as Food and Wine Magazine, Gourmet, and Wine Spectator.

*Opened in August 2002, Woodfire Grill offers a wine-country sensibility with a warm and rustic neighborhood feel. The cuisine is seasonally influenced and ingredient-focused, with a Northern Californian flair.*

I like Michael so much I hired him twice! He showed up in my restaurant, introduced himself and started talking about how much he enjoyed his brunch and how it reminded him of his favorite restaurant in San Francisco, where he grew up. Then he told me about the new restaurant he was opening.

"Where is it?" I asked. When he said it was right next door to Tattletale's, a strip club, I just bit my tongue. Who was I to say anything? When I first opened my restaurant in Virginia-Highland, people probably thought I was crazy too, because of the feel of the neighborhood back then. Later, when I thought back on it, Michael's new restaurant might have been the best location on Piedmont, because everyone knows where Tattletale's is.

I kind of laughed when he came in my restaurant and handed out cards for his restaurant in the months before it opened. My feeling was that the more good restaurant operators there are out there, the better it is for Atlanta. I was young, Michael was young and I wanted to be associated with the new generation of restaurateurs. The group that included Panos Karatassos of Buckhead Life Restaurant Group was too old and too arrogant for us younger folks.

Then Michael opened Chef's Café and took Atlanta by surprise — it was a huge success. At Murphy's we had introduced some dishes to Atlanta that were simple but original, like the croissant sandwich. Michael did the same thing by bringing California cuisine to Atlanta. And I had never had a latte or a cappuccino before I went to Chef's Café.

Michael Tuohy

And talk about a driven individual! Michael is a professional and totally committed to the food industry.

### Michael Tuohy:

"I had two eras at Murphy's. I first went there in the spring of 1996. I was anxious and to some degree, terrified by the food they were serving. They had this huge rack with #10 cans and one of my first moves was to get rid of that thing. I said, 'What do you do with all those cans? Where is your fresh produce?'

Working there was like being at The Murphy Hotel; we were serving three meals a day and it never stopped. We were able to change the menu and get it into place before the Olympics that summer — two of our busiest weeks ever.

For me, the big project for the menu was to get Tom out of the deli mentality. The dinner menu had ten sandwiches on it and I chopped that back to three or four.

I introduced seafood at Murphy's, because the closest thing he had was tuna fish salad. Back then the most expensive entrée was $10.99 and I got him to increase that to $15.99 for salmon. He wanted to add crab cakes but I told him he would have to charge for it. I also got him to add fried calamari. 'Trust me — this will sell,' I said. It did.

The whole evolution of the menu took about a year and a half. We continued evolving after the Olympics, and I got Tom to agree to change the menu seasonally. Some things, like the fettuccine with pesto and portobello mushrooms, were like the Holy Grail — he wouldn't let me touch those.

Tom's dad is a special person and a nice man, but he about drove me nuts with the stuff he would bring to the back door. I'd take a day off work and come back to a cooler full of vinegars and miniature carrot sticks. Tom would say, 'We got a good deal on those. Can't you make something with them?'

But the dish that I will always hold against Tom is The Big Murphy. That was the bane of any chef's existence. I wanted to throw those potatoes against the wall. But they sold like there was no tomorrow.

I also wanted to get rid of the chili. I said to Tom, 'I can't do this. I have to go cook real food.'

In 1997 I left and went to Indigo. Then, in May 2000 I came back, despite the fact that the chili and The Big Murphy were still there. My wife and I had almost moved to Nashville and opened a restaurant there. We decided to stay, but I still wanted my own restaurant, so I consulted for Tom right before I opened Woodfire Grill.

When I came back it was still busy, but had evolved. With the perspective gained by leaving, then returning to Murphy's, I thought it looked noticeably tired. And dinner was not doing as well as it should have been. It needed reenergizing and retooling. The demographic of the neighborhood had shifted somewhat.

That corner of Virginia and North Highland now had La Tavola, Noche, and Fontaine's. Those restaurants were mobbed on the weekend nights and we were emptying out. These people were partying at night — so who wanted to come in to Murphy's and eat cupcakes?

We were only selling wine and beer, and people were constantly asking for mixed drinks. I urged Tom to turn the front to a bar. He resisted the idea and there was a lot of hand wringing on that decision. Tom has to get in his comfort zone and sometimes he will give in to pressure. Hey, he's Irish! (I say that in a good way.)

It seemed that there was always something broken in the kitchen. Tom would haul in something from a warehouse and say, 'Will this work?' I'd look at it and say, 'We have 800 people coming in for brunch. No, that won't work.'

I remember making five gallons of Hollandaise at a time for brunch: 280 eggs and a vat of clarified butter. I had to stand there with a huge hand-held blender and buzz it for 20 minutes. I'd make four different flavors and at 2:30 I'd be praying that I wouldn't run out.

And I'll never forget the Little Zipper Incident. Little Zipper was a steam kettle that could boil water very fast so we could make soups in a hurry. It wasn't 'hard-plumbed' and we had to fill it with water. Every now and then Little Zipper got too excited and would blow. Once we had a prep guy who was standing right next to Little Zipper when she blew. It scared him so bad he wet his pants. He walked out and we never saw him again.

It's amazing the amount of things that can go wrong with that volume and that many people in a hot, wet, electrical environment.

Tom and I became close friends, and he was the best man at our wedding in 1989. The night before the wedding we rented a limo and went out on the town 'Murphy style.' (I'll divulge no more details of that evening.)

In the fall of 2001 after 9-11, business was down and I knew it was time for me to move on to my own restaurant. I already had my vision for Woodfire Grill. If I'm going to be cooking for a living I want to cook what I believe in. Otherwise it's just too hard. Work is so overrated.

So in December of 2001 I left. Woodfire Grill opened in August 2002."

## Hector Santiago, Pura Vida

*Hector Santiago*

Hector Santiago is the chef and owner of Pura Vida Tapas Restaurant, which opened in March 2001. Originally from Puerto Rico, he has a degree in business from the University of Puerto Rico, and is also a graduate of the Culinary Institute of America. Before moving to Atlanta, Hector worked at the renowned Manhattan Ocean Club, was banquet chef at the Four-Star Stony Hill Inn in New Jersey, and was sous chef at the Heartland Brewery. After moving to Atlanta, he worked as executive chef at several of the Peasant Restaurants, as well as Murphy's and Duex Plex, before opening Pura Vida. His varied experience in both catering and a la carte dining, in American, Italian, and French cooking and exposure to *many different ingredients helped to broaden his techniques. His heart and passion, however, remained Latino food.*

*At Pura Vida, which opened in March 2001, Hector serves Latin American and Spanish-inspired food combined with classical cooking techniques.*

Hector Santiago came from one of Bob Amick's restaurants. He was well-trained in organization and had a wonderful palate. He also had a drive to open his own restaurant, which he did, right down the street, thereby increasing the reputation of Virginia-Highland as a restaurant destination.

### Hector Santiago:

"I had been working for Peasant Restaurants when one of the chefs at Murphy's recommended me for a job there. I only worked there for a few months in 1999, during the busy season — although I think it's always the busy season there. The restaurant is not that large, but it has so much business. It always amazed me. I had only been there once because I was living in Marietta and what with working and commuting, I didn't go out much. But I knew its reputation. I had to work like a machine there.

Working there really helped me learn what people look for in food and atmosphere. It was also great getting to know the area. It reminded me of a small village where people walk up and down the street, to work and to eat. I really loved that it was close to the city but had a neighborhood atmosphere.

Learning about the area really helped me when I was looking to open my own restaurant, which is now only about a mile away."

# Bob Amick, ONE. midtown kitchen, TWO. urban licks, piebar

*Bob Amick launched his restaurant career in 1974 with the Peasant Restaurants. He created Mick's Restaurants, named for his father, to appeal to a more casual segment of the industry. After growing the Peasant and Mick's companies to more than 40 restaurants nationally, developing and promoting each individual concept to be the most highly acclaimed restaurants at the time, Bob and his partner sold to Quantum in 1989. Bob stayed on as CEO, taking the company public under Morton's Restaurant Group and later doing a secondary offering. After selling his remaining interests, Bob left to go solo. His first venture was the highly acclaimed Killer Creek, which opened in 1998. Bob sold Killer Creek in 2001, and started the development of a series of high-profile, chef-driven dining experiences in the burgeoning area of Midtown Atlanta.*

*Award-winning ONE. midtown kitchen opened in 2002, and has received local and national accolades for its simple and uncomplicated approach to food, wine, and service. TWO. urban licks, Bob and Company's sequel, is setting the town on fire with wood-roasted meats and fish and a funky, urban edge. Bob opened piebar in the summer of 2005, with two other restaurants to open in 2006.*

*In addition to his restaurants, Bob launched Concentrics Hospitality Solutions in 2002, a full-service restaurant consulting company specializing in concept development.*

Bob Amick has been one of the most influential people in my life.

Working with Bob was like going to Harvard and getting my doctorate in the restaurant business. As a single-unit operator, for years I would ask myself, "What are the big guys thinking?" "Am I doing this the right way?" "What would it be like to run a big operation?"

I got the opportunity to learn all of that by working with Bob, who ran 49 restaurants at once when he worked with Peasant Restaurants. We had an instant bond and his thought process was as entrepreneurial as mine. Bob taught me how to approach things the right way. It's possible I would have made the same decisions without having worked with him, but I had been approaching them in a more emotional way.

I learned from Bob that it requires an enormous amount of energy to stay on top of the game in this industry. Bob still runs circles around restaurateurs half his age. You need to keep the passion and energy, because it is ultimately passed on to your staff and then on to your guests.

## After 25 years, Murphy's is an overnight sensation.
*Bob Amick*

For me, Bob crystallized the concept that a restaurateur has to fill the space he or she is in. Bob has the passion, the ego, and the talent to fill the big spaces.

With Murphy's, Bob took a diamond in the rough and polished it. I could not have done it without his expertise. The biggest lesson I learned from Bob is that if you're not willing to make bold changes, then your destiny is defined.

Bob is a man I could trust and I knew he could run my business better than I could. That is a great feeling after 25 years. The best thing I did was turn the management of Murphy's over to his company, Concentrics Hospitality Solutions. Now I can do what I love — meet and greet people in the restaurant while Bob handles the management.

Thanks, Bob!

*Bob Amick:*

"One day in 2001, Tom Murphy called me and said, 'Are you the Bob Amick of Peasant Restaurants?' When I said yes, he said, 'Let's go to lunch. I have something to talk to you about.'

So we went to lunch and Tom told me that he was in the middle of a reconfiguration of Murphy's, and wanted my help. One thing I've learned about Tom is that when he doesn't have the answers or solutions to something, he finds someone who does. He caught me at a good time because I was taking time off and it was right before I began working on ONE. midtown kitchen.

The first thing I said when he told me what he wanted was, 'You can't afford me.' The second thing was, 'Don't hire me if you don't want to listen. I will be bluntly honest and you'll have to trust me.' So we came to a good arrangement on the front end.

Tom never sits still, which is a negative and a positive. He seldom sits back, complacent with what he has. He has a typical ADD personality, like my son. I'll take my son to an amusement park and while we're riding on one ride, he isn't fully enjoying it because he is thinking about the next ride.

Tom is always worried about how things will play out. But the positive in this is that he is always thinking ahead, making moves like a chess game. And that is what has kept his restaurant from getting stale.

A lot of people come up with a concept and just expect it to roll for 20 years, but Tom doesn't do that. He has the vision, but doesn't always have the technical skills to carry it out himself. But he does know how to find people who can do it for him. Restaurants need reinvigorating. But for whatever reason — lack of knowledge, energy, passion — lots of people lie down and die, or else their ego is so big they say, 'I don't need help.' Tom isn't like that.

Some people don't hire me because I also own restaurants, but I don't worry about competition. If I fail it's because I didn't do something right, not because of what someone else is doing down the street. And if I respect you and your goals, I'm willing to help.

If you own a restaurant and you are there all the time, you become oblivious. You can lose your energy and your creative edge. People forget about you so easily. You're only as good as your last meal. It's crucial to find your staying power. This business is built on passion.

The challenge with changing a restaurant is to keep the old customers but also attract new ones. I hadn't been to the new location and didn't really have a perception of it when I first started working with Tom.

Tom had a history of bringing people through the restaurant for their advice. So when I went in, the staff just looked at me like, 'Here's another one, but he'll be gone soon too.' I knew no one liked me, but I told them, 'I'm not going anywhere.'

Back then, his front room was a mess, with T-shirts hanging on the wall for sale. The look wasn't helping his image and the way it was run was costing him a fortune. One of the hardest parts of my consulting business is that people want to tell you how wonderful their business is. But I have to tell people it's not wonderful.

Tom kept bragging about his desserts and how fantastic they were. Murphy's desserts looked wonderful, but they tasted terrible. Finally one day, I said, 'Tom, shut up. Your desserts are awful and we are going to sit here and eat every one.' So we did. We sat down and tasted every one of his desserts. At the end, he put down his fork and said, 'You're right, they are awful.'

The recipes for the desserts were good originally but either they had been changed or the chefs weren't following them. They were also making the desserts too far ahead, and were freezing some of them.

It was also crucial to add liquor sales. We renovated the front of the restaurant and added a beautiful bar, but Tom was still nervous about serving liquor. When he opened this location he had so much trouble with the neighborhood that he was worried someone might object. I told him that it was not a huge investment for a license, and that if you're moving away from the perception of a breakfast place and want to be a destination dinner place, you couldn't do it by selling wine out of pastry cases.

*Bob Amick and I became good friends as well as business partners. Working with Bob was like getting a doctorate in the restaurant business.*

So we moved the pastry case and hired a new pastry chef, John Hamstra, who is creative and European-trained. He is very talented and a great find for Tom.

We also had to make changes with the staff. The folks who were working for him weren't fans of Murphy's. Sometimes a restaurant can take on a life of its own, and it's not the life you want it to take. Within the first year, we probably turned over 99 percent of the staff. I brought in a lot of people who had worked for me, and we changed the uniforms and the whole culture of the servers' environment. Now, people like working there and are proud to be there. They see an owner who is investing in the place and giving them the tools to do their jobs. This is an industry where people can milk it — take and not give back, and it means a lot to the staff when they see an owner care enough to continue investing in the restaurant.

Although it has changed drastically in the past few years, it is still the same old Murphy's. The key is to make changes gradually, so it's not too different.

Murphy's is an Atlanta icon and was a catalyst for the changes that took place in Virginia-Highland, a great little jewel of an area and one of the few of its kind in Atlanta. Tom fought a lot of battles for his restaurant, but he won them and deserves a lot of credit. Now it's more than a neighborhood restaurant. It has a citywide reputation, and it's a great place for breakfast, lunch, and dinner, or to just drop in for a glass of wine. I eat brunch there every weekend. There isn't a better casual restaurant in the city. The quality is great and they have a wonderful, affordable wine program. You can have great wine and food and not be beaten over the head price-wise. We took it from a deli to a restaurant. And in three years, his sales have gone up 25 percent.

Changing the restaurant is a journey and we're still going through it. Trust can be a funny thing when you own your own business for so long. Tom and I have a great relationship. The biggest thing I've done for Tom is give him back his spirit. He's a completely different person now from when I first met him. I get more pleasure out of that than anything. He has become passionate again.

We just redid the seating plan and the bathrooms. In the long run we'd like to put in a private dining room and a wood-burning oven. In this business you have to keep reinventing yourself just to stay current. We want to continue to raise the bar — not in big jumps but with little steps.

Too many people think restaurants are an art form. This is a business. And when you're doing well is when you have to worry the most. Most restaurants fail because they are under funded, don't have staying power, or didn't have a viable idea to begin with.

One of my goals in life is to tear down the food industry pedestal. A restaurant is social entertainment — that's all. That's why I like Murphy's, because it's accessible. A lot of people are full of hogwash when they talk about food, and especially about wine. It's just juice.

Everyone gets so carried away. To me what's important is what I put in my mouth. Is it good? Is it worth the money? Would you order it again? It doesn't have to be that complicated. A great hamburger is a great hamburger."

# Nick Oltarsh

Nick is one of the great chefs in this country, and in Atlanta in particular. He has a passion for his work and is incredibly organized. When Nick travels around the world, he goes off the beaten track and finds out where flavors originated.

He has brought so much to Murphy's, and elevated the menu to its current level. We have fresh food and a menu that changes with the seasons, with a touch of the South but still very much American eclectic.

Nick is a silent giant, and the best thing about working with him is that no matter what is going on in the kitchen, he is always in control, always teaching and coaching others.

He presents well in public. When he was on TV as part of the show on TBS, "Movie and a Makeover," he was very much at ease with it. He is equally competent in the kitchen or performing onstage in public.

Nick is one of those jewels you just love working with. He is so talented he could open his own place any time. But our chemistry is fantastic and we're having a great time. He even convinced me that the Big Murphy had to go. Murphy's had changed, and that baked potato just didn't fit. That is the beauty of new blood like Nick. It helps you keep yourself fresh.

*Nick Oltarsh:*

"I came to Murphy's in 2002, a few months after moving to Atlanta from New York. I spent the first ten years of my life in Westchester, New York and when I was 10, my parents decided to move back into the city.

I was always interested in cooking and my mom and grandma were great cooks. My parents were foodies and we ate out a lot. I kind of did my education backwards. First I went to University of Pennsylvania, where I was a French literature major. Then I went to the Culinary Institute in Hyde Park, New York. I worked in Manhattan at Eleven Madison Park and Gramercy Tavern but my wife got tired of New York and got herself transferred to Atlanta, right before 9-11.

I was unemployed for three months and then got a job at Eatzi's. I met Gerry Klaskala, who introduced me to Tom, who hired me to come and work at Murphy's.

Murphy's had a great menu when I came. We always have to have a balance to keep the old timers happy, but I wanted to add new items. For example, we still serve meatloaf. I added fried green tomatoes, which is my favorite item, and knew they would sell. They did. I wanted to try new things, like calves liver. It might be a disaster but you don't know until you try it. We added brisket — which is a little out there — but people love it. We serve it with cauliflower, which is known in the industry as a 'kill' item (like Brussels sprouts and rutabaga). They can be delicious, but certain things scare people.

We have our misses too. I once tried a fried shrimp with cream of wheat batter with romescu sauce. I thought because it was fried it would sell, but it didn't catch on.

We do a lot of tweaking and changing. Some things we won't take off the menu, like the fried green tomatoes, but nothing is really untouchable. We had a pasta with pesto on the menu. It was untouchable but we touched it.

The menu was too large, so I contracted it. I took off what didn't sell, then expanded it back by adding different items. I took The Big Murphy off the menu two years ago. Its popularity began to wane in 2001, perhaps due to high-carb worries, and I removed it from the menu to make way for new dishes. People still ask about it.

We change the menu seasonally, about four times a year. I wanted to make the dinner menu more sophisticated. But first, I started with lunch, trying to raise the bar, although people mostly just want sandwiches and salads. And I was more than happy to give it to them. Sometimes it's best not to be too sophisticated. You have to balance it — give people what they want, but teach them what they should want. Every chef brings his own personality to the menu. I like vegetables so I wanted to add as many as I could. Sometimes I hide them in a dish and hope people like it. For our specials, I buy a bunch of interesting vegetables and then figure out what to do with them. Once I tried a chicken with smoked tomato sauce and the combination of sweet, sour, and salty flavors should have worked, but it was awful.

I do all the wording on the menu myself. Sometimes

if I just change a word or two the item will sell better. I have a tarragon biscuit appetizer with ham that doesn't sell well but is delicious. I think if I took out the word 'tarragon' it would do great. And, the higher up on the menu, the better an item sells.

At brunch, Linda's Omelette is always the most popular dish. I don't even know who Linda is. For lunch, it's the half soup/salad/sandwich, which was Bob Amick's idea. At dinner the Grouper with Garlic Shrimp is popular, as is Calamari and Fried Green Tomatoes.

When I first came I had never done brunch and it was a little nerve-wracking. We serve 700 on Saturday and 800 on Sunday — astounding for a restaurant this size. We have three cooks for hot dishes and one for cold, and everything is cooked to order. All of our baked goods are from scratch: one guy makes the biscuits and another makes the muffins. It is a sight to behold.

It is the smoothest service I've ever worked in. These folks have been doing it for so long that all the kinks have been worked out. It is a joy to work — the best a la carte brunch menu I've ever seen anywhere. In New York they charge twice as much and have nothing on us. It is so cool to just watch as hundreds of plates go by. There is one cook who has been doing it for ten years.

What I like about Murphy's is that it's been around forever and is still popular. It is constantly evolving. Tom's best quality is that he is not afraid to take chances and make changes. When you do that with such a popular

*One of my favorite things about owning a restaurant is entertaining our friends. We gave a dinner to celebrate the wedding of Jan Butsch, my co-writer, and Chris Schroder, my publisher! Here are Mike Egan, Mindy Egan, Caroline Bridges, Charles Driebe, Chris and Jan.*

place you risk alienating people, but you have to change if you want to survive. Tom could have coasted but he made investments in the restaurant. He didn't have to do that. That's his key to success.

That's why I've stayed so long, Business has always been great here. It's very casual and neighborhoody. The restaurants I worked at in New York were more formal. The crowd here is very diverse — you have families, the cool crowd, the business crowd, the late-night crowd. There is something for everybody."

# The Dark Side: When Things Go Wrong

Owning a restaurant is like throwing a new party every day. But there is also a risk. The dark side that could make your business disappear. We've had our share of mishaps. One of my sayings is that sometimes it takes experience to gain wisdom. Here are a few of the reasons I'm so wise today.

We try to help the community by hiring people in recovery centers, people in transition. Once we hired a dishwasher, but he didn't work out and we had to get rid of him. One day soon after that, I had worked from 8 a.m. to midnight and went up to my office (to my La-Z-Boy) to sleep. The next morning the restaurant was full and this former dishwasher comes busting in the side entrance and starts screaming "Fire!" Then he pulls over a 16-foot display rack and sent it crashing to the floor. Glass and dishes went flying. Two customers grabbed him and pinned him down. There was a police officer across the street at the fire station and he came over and took the man away. The trauma of the whole ordeal was worse than the expense of replacing that huge case. But it was great to see the customers step in and help. I learned that day that customers become your family *and* your guards.

If there has been in time when I rethought my decision to spend my life in the restaurant industry, it may have been the moment I had a gun pointed at my face.

Ed Thomas was my general manager then, and we were closing the restaurant for the night. There had been a rash of robberies in the neighborhood. While Ed swept the floors and I wiped down the deli counter, we were arguing about whether we should leave the lights on while we closed, or turn them off. Ed was saying we should leave them on so the restaurant looked occupied. I said we should turn them off so we can see out of the windows. So there we were, engaged as we often were in a battle of the wills, neither one wanting to budge an inch.

While we were arguing in the front of the restaurant, three guys carrying guns had walked in through the back door and were robbing our employees. Then they came in the front, and you better believe our argument quit immediately as one of them pulled a gun on me. All of a sudden I had tunnel vision — all I could see was that gun and I could feel the adrenaline pumping through my body.

There were eight of us in the room at that point and one of the gunmen told us all to get on the floor. Then he and his buddies went down the line and stole all of our watches, money, and wallets. Thankfully, they got what they wanted and fled.

The police caught the guys, and Ed went to testify against them. They went to jail. We never got our stuff back but we did have insurance to cover our losses. The main thing is that although our stuff was stolen, no one was hurt. But let's just say the episode was one of the low points of my career.

The amazing thing is that we all went back to work the next day and just continued working. That's the thing about the restaurant business — you move from one crisis to another without much time to dwell on any one incident! I'll be a happy man though, if I never have to see a gun pointed at me again.

On a lighter note, one day we showed up for work at the first location and all our tables, which were made from spools, had disappeared from the patio. An anonymous caller told us told us to check at The Cove, which was a rundown, late-night gay bar north of Piedmont Park. We went to check it out, and sure enough, there were our tables. We never found out who the caller was or how they recognized those stools as belonging to Murphy's.

Another time, we showed up one morning and the safe was gone, with $10,000 from the weekend gone with it, and one of our dishwashers had disappeared. There was also a long metal tool missing that was used to screw down bar stools. Looks like we had a suspect. I called the police, reported the incident and gave them the address of the dishwasher. They told me they had arrested a man the night before for DUI and had impounded his car. There was no safe in the car but they did find the metal tool. So they got a warrant to go to his house. They found the dishwasher, sitting there with a hammer trying to open the safe. We got all of the money back.

After we started the catering division and the business continued to grow, we had three different checking accounts. I hired a Georgia State grad who was sitting for his CPA boards to help out as a bookkeeper. I wrote checks for everything so I had huge statements. I was taking in a lot of money then, but there never seemed to be enough and I could barely pay my taxes. So I decided to go through one of my statements to see how long it took for a check to clear, just so I would know how much float I would have.

What I found made me sick. I found four checks for a total of $3000 made out to him. I was stunned. And that was just for the month of December. I went back through the statements for a year and found that he had written checks to himself for $35,000. No wonder I could barely pay my taxes.

I called him in the next morning. He confessed and said he needed the money because he was getting married, and thought he could borrow it, and then pay me back. I was completely shell-shocked and felt really violated. He had seemed like the nicest guy — $35,000 worth of nice.

He promised to pay me back. And I believed him. (Lesson learned: After you find someone stealing from you, chances are good he is lying when he says he will pay you back.) The next day he didn't show up for work, so I called the police. Eventually I found out he had first hightailed it to

Mexico, then gotten a job in Texas.

Two weeks later I got a phone call. It was his sister and she told me her brother was in town, but that he would be leaving soon and she was having a party for him. "Would you make the cake?" she asked. I was stunned. It was obvious he had not shared the details of his departure from Murphy's with her.

"Of course," I said. It's not every day you get to make a "Thanks for the Embezzlement" cake.

So I called Eldrin Bell, who was then chief of police, to let him know about the party. I met the sister at her beauty salon

*Shopping List*
*One Weekend of Brunch*

*80 pounds of bacon*

*10 gallons of grits*

*400 cartons of eggs*

*360 pounds of potatoes*

*15 gallons of pancake batter*

*32 gallons of orange juice*

*1000 biscuits and 1000 muffins*
*(which we cook over the course of the day)*

and got a deposit and her address so I could "deliver the cake."

It was a surprise party, all right, but probably not quite the type they had planned. The police showed up and arrested my former employee at the party. Now *that's* an event to remember.

We had a female district attorney who prosecuted the case. She took a special interest in it because her husband had also been embezzled from. My former employee pleaded guilty.

The judge said, "I sentence you to death." Now even I was thinking that was a wee bit harsh for the crime. I looked quizzically at the judge, as did everyone else in the courtroom. "That's my favorite place and you could have closed it down!" she said. He escaped the death penalty, but she ordered him to jail. He paid me back quarterly when he got out and I eventually got all my money back.

*Mary Barber Cox is a loyal customer and made this beautiful illustration for me. She is the mother of Georgia Secretary of State Cathy Cox.*

# Customers

Katie Couric used to come in about once a week when we were at our old location. I had a big crush on her and when she walked in I always smiled. She was such a cute all-American girl, cute as a bug. That's the kind of girl I like — so spunky and smart. I wonder if she remembers us.

We've had our share of celebrities in here, but that was never what my place was about. What sticks in my mind more are stories about my everyday customers.

One morning I was in the restaurant before we were open and a car came zooming up. A guy jumped out and started beating on the window. "Open up," he was yelling. I opened the door and he said, "My wife is about to have a baby and we're on the way to the hospital and she's craving some honey wheat doughnuts." I ran back and grabbed a bag for him. I wanted people to have Murphy's as part of their lives every day, but that seemed a bit much, even for me.

A few years back I saw a mom and son having lunch one day. I walked over to them and said, "It is really nice to see a mother and son enjoying time together. I'd like to buy you a dessert." A year later I was at a wonderful Vietnamese restaurant named Nam having dinner with my son. A lady walked over and said, "You don't remember me, but I'd like to buy you a dessert." That's right — it was the same lady and she remembered me.

You've already heard several stories from Murphy's customers. Here are few more:

"The night before my wedding our rehearsal dinner was down the street at Atkins Park. We had a lovely time but had no dessert. Several guests ventured out to get ice cream, but I was instructed to *GO TO BED*. I was staying at Ponce Place Bed and Breakfast and *HAD* to pass Murphy's on my way. I stopped and got a slice of Bonzo cake to go. I luxuriated in a hot bubble bath, wearing my tiara, sipping champagne and eating my Bonzo cake! It was *PERFECT* and one of my favorite 'I'm a princess!' stories."

*Angie Wehunt*

"In 1994, I was dating Mary, a gal from Mississippi. She was in Atlanta on a special temporary assignment, which was about to end. On August 8, she told me that she had accepted a permanent position in Atlanta, not one she really wanted but she wanted to stay. I asked her to join me for dinner at Murphy's on Wednesday, August 10, the last night before she returned home to prepare for the move.

When we arrived at Murphy's, I secretly enlisted the assistance of our server to help me with a plan I had devised. With each course of the meal, our waitress brought to the table a note with a small gift, presumably from another patron in the restaurant. Mary was much impressed and I feigned outrage at such behavior, claiming she must be doing something to attract such attention.

Finally, when dessert came, it appeared to me that my position with Mary had been so shaken that I must take some dramatic action in response to the other male patrons. So, I pulled out a note and package of my own and handed it to her. Of course, the note said how much I loved her and the package contained an engagement ring. Fortunately, she said 'Yes!' We got married on August 26th and have lived happily ever since.

We still come to Murphy's on many special occasions and it will always hold a special place in our memories for that night. And, the food is always good, too."

*Larry Wilson*

*Larry Wilson proposed to his wife Mary with a special dinner at Murphy's, which has been the site for many proposals and celebrations.*

"When I was thirteen I rode a motorbike from my home in Druid Hills to Murphy's (when it was on Los Angeles). On the way back home I received a ticket for driving a motorized vehicle on a public street under age. Ten years later I discovered Murphy's chili potpie in the potato crust. It was the best I ever had."

*Joshua Goldfarb*

"My husband, Benjy, took me to Murphy's on our first date a little over seven years ago. Over the next several years we continued to patronize Murphy's on a regular basis, including a re-creation of our first date, one year to the date after we started dating. Last year my co-workers took me out to lunch right before our wedding, I thought it was very fitting that my co-workers selected the place that Benjy and I shared our first date. We were married last year in Atlanta, and had several out-of-town guests fly in for the weekend. Of course Murphy's was listed in our wedding weekend restaurant list and many guests took us up on our suggestion to dine at Murphy's.

I hope Murphy's will continue to be around for as long as I live; I love the thought of being able to visit the place where Benjy and I have shared, and will continue to share many memories."

*Cynthia Mokotoff*

*Tom and Landria O'Rourke are good friends of ours, shown here getting in the spirit of things at our St. Patrick's Day dinner.*

"Shortly before the birth of my first child, some dear friends of mine hosted a baby brunch for me at Murphy's. They were all good friends I had worked with at the Atlanta Committee for the Olympic Games. Great girlfriends, great food, lovely gifts."

*Carol Milliron*

"When Murphy's was in the former location, down the street from the fire station, I took my young son Wes, who was four in 1983, to Murphy's on Saturday morning for breakfast. It became a Saturday morning ritual that we would look forward to — a trip to Murphy's and a visit to see the bulldog at the fire station. A little lady from across the street used to bake biscuits and muffins and bring them over to Murphy's. I could not believe how 'down home' this intown Atlanta restaurant felt!

I followed Murphy's to the new location (which is where I used to buy our Christmas tree when it was a vegetable and health foods stand). I wish Wes were still here to see how you have grown and prospered. He died one month before his 20th birthday. Among my treasured memories of him were our Saturdays spent at Murphy's. Murphy's will always hold a special place in my heart and so will Tom and his family."

*Bonnie Stephens Wolf*

"I moved to Atlanta in 1990, mostly because I was seeing a lady who lived here. Soon after I moved, this lady (who is now my wife) suggested we have dinner at Murphy's. The restaurant was in the original location at that time. As I recall, diners had to go behind the deli counter and climb a set of somewhat narrow stairs to get to the dining tables. It was a cozy place, a bit unusual, and very good food. It quickly became one of our favorite restaurants and the Virginia-Highland area, which I discovered through going to Murphy's, became a favorite destination.

After Murphy's moved to its current location, we would always buy some of the deli salads and desserts during our trips to dine at Murphy's. We miss the deli counter, but understand that times change. In fact, Murphy's has been very perceptive in changing along with (perhaps even leading) the changing character

*John and Junith Koon*

and personality of the Virginia-Highland area. Murphy's remains a favorite restaurant — because the food and wine are consistently good and because of the memories we have of our developing relationship together at Murphy's."

*John Koon*

*Our daughter, Katherine and her friends from King O'Sullivan Dance School, came to dance for our customers on St. Patrick's Day.*

"My dear friend Marla Eastwood and I went to Vietnam, Cambodia, and Thailand to celebrate the millennium. As we landed in Hartsfield Airport after weeks of trekking through Southeast Asia, with Marla's tummy still turning from a week of unresolved dysentery, Marla and I turned to each other and said 'Murphy's veggie chili.' Yum!"

*Julianna Evans*

"I've been eating with Tom Murphy since before he had a restaurant called Murphy's. I came to Atlanta as a medical student in the late seventies. I was doing rotations at Grady Hospital and just couldn't eat in the cafeteria. So I'd go out to the Municipal Market. There were a number of stands there and one guy with a small bread and cheese stand where I would buy a sandwich, then go eat outside in a small green space and feel fairly human, eating nice food.

Then when Tom opened his restaurant I was living over by Emory and went to brunch there, and sometimes for dinner. About 10 years ago, I moved to Virginia-Highland and now I can walk to Murphy's. Virginia-Highland is one neighborhood where you can still do that.

I owned a business called Innovations, and we would go out for lunch. Almost every day we went to Murphy's. I shudder to think how much money I've spent there over the years. It was the one place that was truly casual, a neighborhood place. When the servers saw us, they would just set down a whole pitcher of iced tea. We drank a lot of iced tea.

After all those years I knew Tom by sight, but we didn't really know each other. Innovations did a lot to support the organization CARE and we hosted benefits. Tom came one time and bought $500 worth of raffle tickets, then handed them out to my staff. That's when I started to see another side of Tom. He is obviously a guy who is tuned into doing good and has feelings of social responsibility. That made me even happier to eat at Murphy's.

Then in the summer of 2000, I discovered I had brain cancer. I was in the hospital awhile. Tom heard about this from one of my staff and insisted on getting food together for my family. When I got out of the hospital, he wanted to know if I had a craving for anything because he knew that sometimes happens when you're undergoing chemotherapy. Michael Tuohy was working there then and they both said, 'Whatever you want, we'll get it to you.' Tom and I didn't even really know each other but he dropped food off for me.

When I travel, he always wants to take me to the airport. He will often come and pick me up to go to lunch. These things just show the kind of person he is. I still eat there a lot. One of my friends always orders the chicken spinach burger so the servers don't even ask for his order.

I like the food but I also like that they do change it occasionally. It would have gotten a little boring after eating there for more than 20 years."

*Craig White*

"When my son was three or four months old we stopped by Murphy's for lunch. He was cranky and fussy and I didn't want to breastfeed in public. We gave him garlic smashed potatoes, which he loved. He hadn't had solid food before that, but he quieted down long enough for my husband and me to get fed as well."

*Terri Thornton*

"The best thing about Murphy's is that our favorite foods have stayed on the menu for many years. Murphy's has gently evolved over the years, rather than having to periodically re-invent itself — and that is a feat. We always take our out-of-town guests to Murphy's on Sunday mornings on our way to the airport. When these out-of-towners come back they always say 'We are going to Murphy's for Sunday breakfast, right?'"

*J.B. Booth*

"I lived in Virginia-Highland in the late eighties, at the corner of Amsterdam and Monroe and was a frequent diner at Murphy's. Sunday brunches were a favorite! Now, every time I come back to Atlanta, Murphy's is a must-stop."

*Laura Peet,*
*New York City*

John Walraven

"Michael Tuohy did my engagement party in the far-right section of the dining room on a Saturday night in the spring of '02. It was a masterpiece. A five-course tapas menu with paired wines. We had 36 people crammed in there and downed 29 bottles of wine. It was a madhouse. Everybody had a blast and everybody remembers it as a fun time. It was indeed the best part of that engagement, which failed a few months before the big day. I'll never forget that one and think that my former fiancée would concur."

*John Walraven*

"When I think of Murphy's, I think elegant and cosmopolitan. I also think of comfort, which isn't always synonymous with the previous two words. It's a place that seems to suit almost every occasion: birthdays, graduations, and other gatherings with close family and friends; business meetings; casual after-work drinks with work acquaintances; Saturday brunch with your boyfriend. It always seems appropriate and places like that are unusual."

*Shani St. John*

"For at least the past 20 years my wife Beverly and I have been eating at Murphy's. On one occasion while we were eagerly awaiting our desserts, Beverly and a couple of our friends were sitting to my left at Murphy's counter. A friendly couple sat to my right. We struck up a pleasant conversation and told them what great desserts Murphy's serves. Several minutes later when my Tollhouse Pie came, I took a bite and remarked to my wife how delicious it was. I then took a spoon and scooped a huge portion of my dessert, turned to my right, put the spoon in the face of the lady sitting next to me, and asked her to sample this wonderful dessert. To my astonishment the other couple had left, and I realized I had my spoon in the face of some strange lady I had never seen before in my life. Needless to say, I had pie in my face the rest of the evening."

*Steve Cole*

*After a hard day of play at the Cunard Memorial Playground down the street, Derek Rizzi likes to refuel with the fish sticks at Murphy's. "I love how fast they get my food to me," he says.*

"In the mid nineties, during our first visit to Atlanta, our daughter and soon-to-be son-in-law, Susanne and Pal Duke took us to Murphy's for lunch. The service and our meals were just wonderful. We still remark that our lunch was the finest food we have ever tasted. In magazines, we always check to see that Murphy's is part of the 'Best' lists. We feel proud to always find Murphy's on the list and we feel part of the Murphy family!"

*Patricia & Tom Dew,*
*Richmond, Virginia*

"I remember Murphy's at the old location, by the firehouse on North Highland. I've been eating there for over twenty years. Atlanta has a national reputation as a great city for brunch, and Murphy's is always at the top of the list. I've seen people waiting for nearly two hours to get in on a Sunday morning. They gather outside to talk with their friends, drink coffee, or visit the other shops in the area, never seeming to mind the wait. In fact, I've never heard anyone complain — no doubt because the food is so good."

*John Companiotte*

*John Companiotte and Catherine Lewis eat at Murphy's several times a week. They enjoy a meal at the bar while chatting with Derrick Turner.*

"I ate dinner at Murphy's the night I gave birth to my first child. The only thing I wanted was Murphy's macaroni and cheese. Little did I know that I would be eating mac and cheese for years to come! I never go into Murphy's now without remembering that night."

*Gillian Temple*

"I've been going to Murphy's since I was an under-graduate at Emory University, and I've lived within a mile of the restaurant ever since. Now we have a house on Lanier Boulevard barely a block away. We walk past it every morning with our two dogs, Blue and Smilla, and we eat there all the time with friends and family. In fact, I think of Murphy's as an extension of my kitchen. After a long day, when we don't want to cook or haven't had time to go to the grocery store, John and I will walk over to Murphy's and sit at the counter. We'll order a good glass of wine and a quick bite — a salad and appetizer and then split a dessert.

When we first moved to our house on Lanier, our friends would call on Sunday morning to ask me to put their name on the waiting list. I would run over in my tennis shoes and shorts, then come home, shower, read the paper, and meet them later for brunch. As you can imagine, we're very popular.

One Sunday, probably three years ago, Murphy's had an almond muffin on the brunch menu, and it was incredible. I'm an avid baker, but these were the best I've ever had — light, fluffy, and not too sweet. I asked the waitress if the chef would give me the recipe. By the time our check came, he had written it out longhand, converting it so I wouldn't have to make a thousand at a time. No doubt, they went through that many each morning. I know how busy the whole staff was, and I was impressed that he took the time to accommodate my mundane request."

*Catherine Lewis*

# Family

I have deservedly given a lot of credit to a lot of folks for the success of Murphy's. But I could never have become a successful restaurateur all these years without the support of my family. It's time for them to have a few words. On the following pages are their thoughts on being related to a restaurant owner.

## Susan Murphy

"As I've mentioned, we both felt our marriage would work better if I didn't work in the restaurant with Tom, but I like to think I've been supportive of him all along.

One of the best things about being married to a restaurant owner is that we enjoy going out as a family and trying different food. He has made us all into foodies. We've also met many, many nice people in this business.

After a renovation to our house in July 2003, we hosted the most amazing dinner with some of the best chefs in the state. We had Nicolas Bour of Iris, Michael Tuohy of Woodfire Grill, Jason Hill of Wisteria, Jamie Adams of Veni Vidi Vici, Elizabeth Terry of Elizabeth's on 37th in Savannah, Greg Herndon of Tiburon Grille, and Gerry Klaskala and Kathryn King of Aria. I just sat back, drank a glass of wine and watched these amazingly talented people. In my own home! Now, *there's* a benefit of being married to a restaurant owner.

We also interviewed pastry chefs at our house. Tom was replacing the former chef so he couldn't conduct interviews at the restaurant. The chef would come to

*Some of the most famous chefs in Atlanta came to our house and cooked dinner in our kitchen. The menu included pan-seared Hudson Valley foie gras; Maine lobster and peeky toe crab salad; Vidalia onion crusted jumbo gulf shrimp; honey lacquered magret duck, rosemary roasted eye of the ribeye and caramelized Georgia fig tart. Just another dinner at the Murphy household.*

our home and make five or six things, then we had to taste them all. Finally, I said, 'Tom, I just can't do this every night.' One night he told me that John Hamstra, our current pastry chef, was coming over. I said, 'I hope you hire him because I can't do this any more.'

The minute I tasted John's truffle, I said, 'This is the man.' I think he is the best pastry chef in the city. I didn't mind all the tastings that night.

We've had our share of not-so-nice people as well. Tom had a manager who was stealing pots and pans and even turkeys from him, sneaking them out in garbage bags.

Then there was a man who lived near the restaurant who would call us every night at 2:00 or 3:00 a.m. to complain that the garbage truck was at the restaurant. We finally had to take our name out of the phone book and were unlisted for years.

And the hours for a restaurant owner are unbelievable. Tom often worked 18 to 20 hours a day. When we had children, I finally put my foot down about Sunday. That was family day and it has been his only day off as long as we've been married. It really is a crazy life and the hours are better suited to young people. That is one reason it was so important to me to stay home with the kids. It's too crazy to have two full-time careers and try to be there for your children. The divorce rate in the restaurant industry is incredibly high.

I used to tell him, 'It's like living with a doctor, but you don't make that kind of money. You're on call all the time.' Murphy's is his first baby, his first-born.

When we opened the first location of Murphy's we knew the neighborhood was going to blossom. It was unique that we were able to grow with the neighborhood. I wish we had invested in real estate back then. The area has gotten more popular and trendy. Our first house was in the neighborhood and we loved it, but one of our best moves was leaving the area. After our third child was born we couldn't stay in the home we were in, and really couldn't afford a bigger house in the area. I

didn't want to move, but after we did, once Tom came home for the evening he stayed. We were just far enough away that he wouldn't go back after the kids went to bed.

My advice to someone who is thinking of marrying a restaurant owner? It's wonderful, but don't work with him. Just be supportive. I suggest not having your family work in the business either. Our kids help out at the restaurant sometimes and it's been a great experience. But it's too cushy for them. I want them to find their own way.

I think people don't understand how hard it is to be an entrepreneur. The competition in the restaurant business is intense. I believe having just one restaurant really helped Tom to be successful. He has been able to nurse it endlessly.

Tom also donates to charity more than anybody I know. He has always been generous and helped all the schools, sports teams and just about anyone else who asks. It probably drives our CPA crazy.

But I have no regrets. I think we're lucky and we count our blessings."

# *Would you go into the restaurant business?*

*Patrick Murphy, 19:*
"If I went into it I'd want to be the investor."

*Kevin Murphy, 17:*
"I'd be really involved. I'd have a lot of restaurants."

*Katherine Murphy, 11:*
"I'd find fun restaurants that had been closed down and turn them into funky restaurants where parents and children could hang out together."

*Patrick Murphy, 19:*

"Having your dad own a restaurant is wonderful. There is always tons of food and some great eating. And we went to the best places on vacation. Here is the secret: Going to wonderful places and eating the great food is called 'Research and Development' so we could order whatever we wanted from the menu. We each got our own appetizers, entrees, and desserts.

It's been great for me to bring dates to Murphy's when money is scarce. I also bring my guy friends here because they love it. We come here for prom and homecoming with our dates and my dad gives us a fixed-price menu.

I bussed tables for a while, worked in salad prep, and also worked in accounting. I got paid better in accounting, but didn't like the work. I was stapling and alphabetizing thousands of papers.

I do the Christmas and New Year's decorations every year. We have a tree and 3000 lights, along with massive ornaments. I've also worked every Thanksgiving for years, assembling the bags and handing out the preordered Thanksgiving dinners. It's a long day but it's fun.

One year I had an accident in my car and my dad said I had to pay for the damage. I got the idea to pull out his hot dog cart and sell hot dogs at our neighborhood pool, which didn't have a concession stand. My dad made me do a full business plan for the hot dog stand.

I sold hot dogs for two years. It was the ultimate summer job. I made a lot of money and I got all the hot dogs I wanted. I ate a minimum of six a day and always ate the first hot dog of the day and the last hot dog of the day. If it was raining and no one was at the pool, I wouldn't go. People called my house to see if I would be at the pool. Some days I served a ton of people and some days, no one."

*Kevin Murphy, 17*

"My dad owning a restaurant is awesome. It's always lively and fun to go there.

One of my earliest memories is of my dad coming home every day with the wine corks. I collected them and had a huge basket full of them when I was six. I also loved coming here because we got to eat for free and I felt like I was the boss.

I worked in the bakery and made desserts and bread. Once Katherine and I pitted cherries and our hands were stained for weeks. We never did that again. I also help my brother with the Thanksgiving dinners, carrying the meals to people's cars.

I remember the construction when dad was moving to this new location. We used to play in the sand and I found a toy airplane. I thought the new place was going to be a little pastry shop but it turned out a lot bigger than I thought.

I go to Murphy's with my friends whenever there is a big game. We eat there then go next door to Taco Mac and watch the game."

*Katherine Murphy, 11*

"I love having a dad who owns a restaurant. You get free drinks and free food. You can also eat all the chocolate you want when no one is looking.

All the people at Murphy's are sweet and kind and they are nice to you. Everybody at Murphy's is wonderful.

I've made cakes with the pastry chef and one time I cracked 100 eggs. John Hamstra is shy but if you poke him he'll brighten up and start laughing. He made me a white chocolate tiara for my birthday. I brought ten Girl Scout friends here and we made truffles. My friends always ask if they can come bake with me. One time when I was in first grade I brought a friend and we got calamari. She asked me what it was but I said, 'Just eat it.' She did and she loved it. I told her later it was squid. Now when friends spend the night they want to go to Murphy's and eat calamari.

I am in an Irish Dance group and we perform at Murphy's on St. Patrick's Day. It is really fun. Sometimes my dad wears a green Afro wig and he'll get up and dance.

My mom always calls Murphy's "The Shop" because it started as a wine and cheese shop. When I was little I called it Weinie Hut Junior because my dad worked with the hot dog stand when he was little. Now I just call it Murphy's."

# Final Thoughts

For me, the definition of a successful restaurant is one that can pay its bills and give enough return so the owner can sustain his family's lifestyle. That is a successful restaurant. Some restaurants can pay their bills, but the families don't do well. We've been lucky that Murphy's is a successful restaurant.

People sometimes ask me why I never opened a second restaurant. One reason is that I worked so hard that psychologically I was unable to do another one. This turned out to be a blessing. I believe by being a single unit I always had the edge over multi units even though they had bigger pockets.

Once my son Patrick asked me why I didn't have more restaurants, like the father of one of his teammates on the soccer team. I said, "Patrick, have you ever seen his dad at any of the soccer games?" He said, "No." I said, "That's one reason I never opened another restaurant."

I have always felt like I was a rookie in this business. It's 25 years later and I have a sense of gratitude for what I've accomplished but I recognize I'm still a rookie. If I ever feel I'm not a rookie, it'll be time to get out. So here's to 25 more years of feeding folks at Murphy's. I hope you'll be one of them.

---

"I have so many great memories but one sticks out in my mind. It's the day I went shopping for my wedding dress. It was January 24th when my five of my closest girlfriends and I set out for a day of shopping to find the perfect dress. The morning was spent trying on dresses and drinking láttes but the last stop of the day was a little dress shop called LaRaine's in Virginia-Highland. It had already been decided in my mind that we would be lunching at my favorite restaurant, Murphy's, which was right down the street.

We were seated where three small cafe tables had been pulled together and were overlooking the center of the restaurant. The room had that warm glow that Murphy's has during the afternoon when sunlight pours in through the windows. As always at that time of day, Murphy's was buzzing with Saturday afternoon brunchers. As we pored over the menu, some of us sipped mimosas and everyone feasted on warm biscuits and muffins that we smothered with butter.

Over the course of the meal we talked about the big day to come and of course all the dresses I had tried on that day. For one moment I was silent as the girls talked and laughed. As I looked around at everyone I thought to myself how wonderful this day had been and how being at Murphy's on such a special occasion was so fitting. The perfect day, with my closest friends, at the perfect place."

*Melanie Snow*

# Recipes

The recipes from Murphy's were developed and reconfigured for home use by Executive Chef Nick Oltarsh, except where noted. These chefs, all of whom have worked for or with Murphy's, also generously contributed recipes of their own.

Rob Atherholt, Crescent Moon

Alon Balshan, Alon's Bakery & Market

Shaun Doty, Table 1280

Gerry Klaskala, Aria

Hector Santiago, Pura Vida

Michael Tuohy, Woodfire Grill

# Brunch & Lunch

# Murphy's Breakfast Bruschetta

**Serves 4**

8 extra-large eggs
Salt and freshly ground black pepper
4 thick slices good-quality farm bread
1 tablespoon unsalted butter
About $1/2$ cup cream cheese, or creamy goat cheese, for smearing
1 ripe heirloom tomato, cut into thick slices
$1/2$ pint red or yellow cherry or teardrop tomatoes, halved
2 tablespoons finely chopped fresh basil leaves

In a bowl, beat together the eggs with salt and pepper to taste, until smooth. Toast or grill the bread slices until golden, and keep warm in a low oven.

Place a large, non-stick skillet over medium heat and add the butter. When the butter has foamed and the foam is beginning to subside, add the egg mixture and scramble to your desired degree of doneness.

Smear the cream cheese on the warm toasted bread and place each slice on a plate; cover each slice with a slice of heirloom tomato.

Season the tomatoes to taste with salt and pepper, and top the tomatoes with the scrambled eggs, dividing them evenly. Scatter with halved cherry tomatoes and basil, and serve immediately.

A great seasonal frittata that simply speaks of what tastes great during the summertime. Frittatas are very neutral in flavor, and take beautifully to many different flavor pairings.

*— Nick*

# Asparagus and Cherry Tomato Frittata

### Serves 2

2 thin spears asparagus
4 large eggs
1 tablespoon heavy cream
$^1/_2$ tablespoon unsalted butter
1 generous tablespoon soft goat cheese, such as Chavrie, divided into small bits
5 cherry tomatoes, washed and halved
1 tablespoon julienned fresh basil leaves
Sea salt and freshly ground black pepper
Extra-virgin olive oil, for drizzling

Preheat the oven to 350°. Cut or break off the bottom 1 inch of each spear and discard. Peel the asparagus from the half-way point down to the bottom. Prepare an ice bath (a bowl of water and ice) and place near the stove. To cook the asparagus, bring a frying pan of salted water to a rapid boil. Drop in the asparagus and cook for 2 to 3 minutes or until just tender. With tongs, transfer the spears to the ice water to quickly stop the cooking. Remove from the ice water and cut into 3-inch pieces on an angle.

In a bowl, beat together the eggs and cream vigorously. Place a small (6-inch works best), non-stick ovenproof skillet over medium heat and add the butter. When the butter has foamed, add the egg mixture to the pan and move the eggs around a bit with a heat-resistant spatula. Push the cooked eggs towards the center of the pan while tilting the pan (this will allow the uncooked eggs to fill in the empty space). When the frittata is firm on the bottom but still slightly liquid on top, place the asparagus, bits of goat cheese, and tomatoes on top and season to taste with salt and pepper. Place the pan in the oven for 2 minutes, or until the vegetables are heated through and the top of the frittata is firm. Remove from oven and slide onto a plate. Sprinkle with the basil and drizzle with a little olive oil. Cut into halves or wedges and serve at once.

# Chicken and Spinach Burgers

Serves 4

1 tablespoon vegetable oil
$1/2$ onion, finely chopped (about 1 $1/2$ cups)
2 strips uncooked, smoked bacon, finely chopped
1 $1/2$ pounds ground chicken (white meat only)
$1/2$ pound frozen spinach, thoroughly thawed and squeezed firmly to get rid of as much water as humanly possible
$1/4$ cup heavy cream
$1/2$ cup dry breadcrumbs
Sea salt and freshly ground black pepper
Cayenne pepper

**To assemble:**
4 split and toasted Kaiser rolls
Mayonnaise
Sliced or shredded lettuce
Sliced tomato
Sliced Swiss cheese

In a skillet, heat the oil and sauté the onions until tender, about 5 minutes. Set the pan aside until the onions are completely cool.

In a bowl, combine the bacon and ground chicken and mix together thoroughly. (This may be accomplished best with (clean) hands.)

Add and mix in the cooled onions, cream, and breadcrumbs, and season to taste with salt, black pepper, and cayenne. Form the mixture into four 8-ounce patties.

Preheat a griddle pan or very large skillet to medium-high heat. Griddle the burgers until done through and firm to the touch (slice gently if you are not sure when the chicken is cooked), 4 to 5 minutes on each side.

Serve on the toasted rolls with mayonnaise, lettuce, tomatoes, and Swiss cheese, in the quantities desired.

# Linda's Omelet

### Serves 1

4 large eggs
1 tablespoon heavy cream
Salt and freshly ground black pepper
1 tablespoon vegetable oil
1 tablespoon finely diced onion
$^1/_2$ cup thinly sliced white mushrooms
1 cup baby spinach leaves, very well washed and spun dry
$^1/_2$ cup shredded extra-sharp cheddar cheese

In a bowl, beat the eggs with the cream until smooth, and add a good pinch of salt and some pepper.

Place a 6-inch, non-stick skillet over low heat and add the oil. When it is hot, add the onions, mushrooms, and spinach and cook, stirring, for 3 minutes. The vegetables should be slightly wilted.

Add the egg-cream mixture to the pan. At first, move the eggs around with a heat-resistant spatula, pushing the cooked eggs towards the center of the pan to let the uncooked eggs flow out to the edges.

Continue cooking until the omelet is cooked through. Spread the shredded cheese on the top, and immediately fold the omelet onto a plate.

This dish was on the menu when I came to Murphy's.
Mexican flavors lend themselves well to egg cookery.
Note: A slurry is a mixture of raw starch and cold liquid, used for thickening.
— *Nick*

# Spicy Eggs Santa Fe

Serves 6

**Sauce (Yield: 2 1/2 cups):**

- 1 tablespoon unsalted butter
- 1/4 cup coarsely chopped onion
- 1 stalk celery, coarsely chopped
- 1 small green pepper, stemmed, seeded, and coarsely chopped
- 1 teaspoon finely chopped garlic
- 1/4 teaspoon cayenne pepper
- Salt
- 16-ounce can plum tomatoes, drained and coarsely chopped
- 1 cup chicken stock, preferably homemade
- 1 tablespoon corn starch
- 2 tablespoons water
- 1 tablespoon chopped cilantro

**For the eggs:**

- 10 large eggs
- 3 tablespoons heavy cream
- Salt and freshly ground black pepper
- 1 tablespoon vegetable oil
- 1/4 cup finely chopped onion
- 1/4 cup finely chopped red pepper
- 1/4 cup finely chopped green pepper
- 1 cup shredded extra-sharp cheddar cheese
- 6 (10-inch) flour tortillas, warmed
- 6 tablespoons sour cream, for garnish
- Whole fresh cilantro leaves, for garnish

To make the sauce: Place a large, heavy saucepan over medium-high heat and add the butter. When it has melted, add and sauté the onion, celery, green pepper, garlic, and cayenne for 3 minutes, stirring. Add 1 teaspoon salt, the tomatoes, and chicken stock and bring to a boil. In a cup, whisk the cornstarch and water together with a fork until smooth. Slowly stir into the simmering tomato mixture, stirring all the time, and cook until the sauce is nicely thickened, about 5 minutes. Stir in the cilantro and remove from the heat, cover, and keep warm while you prepare the eggs.

For the eggs:

In a bowl, whisk together the eggs and cream until smooth, and season with $1/2$ teaspoon salt and $1/2$ teaspoon pepper.

Place a 12-inch nonstick pan over low heat and add the oil. Add the onions and the red and green peppers and cook for 3 minutes, stirring occasionally. Add the egg-cream mixture and the cheddar cheese to the pan. Move the eggs around with a heat-resistant spatula as they begin to set. Continue until the eggs are cooked through.

Place a tortilla on each plate and divide the eggs among the tortillas, placing them in a line down the center. Roll the tortillas up, around the eggs, and drizzle with the hot sauce. Garnish with sour cream and cilantro leaves, and serve.

# Shrimp and Grits

### Serves 4

1 1/2 pounds medium shrimp (16/20 count), peeled and deveined

2 tablespoons finely chopped chipotle chile en adobo (available where Hispanic ingredients are sold; include some of the juice from the can)

1 1/2 tablespoons Old Bay seasoning

1 teaspoon Cajun seasoning

1 tablespoon finely chopped garlic

1/2 cup vegetable oil

1 teaspoon fresh thyme leaves

4 portions cooked instant grits, hot (cooked according to the instructions on the package)

2 tablespoons unsalted butter

1 cup Tomato Lemon Fondue (see page 158)

In a large non-reactive bowl, combine the shrimp and the chipotle puree, Old Bay and Cajun seasonings, garlic, oil, and thyme leaves. Toss to mix evenly, cover, and refrigerate for 8 hours. Bring to room temperature for 20 minutes before proceeding with the recipe.

Remove the shrimp from the marinade with a slotted spoon. Warm 4 shallow bowls in a low oven and make the grits, if you have not already done so.

In a large skillet, warm the butter over medium heat. When the butter is hot but has not yet browned, add the shrimp and sauté for 3 to 4 minutes, turning over as necessary, until firm and pink.

Divide the hot grits among the bowls and spoon some of the shrimp and their cooking liquid over the grits. Top with about 1/4 cup of the tomato-lemon fondue and serve at once.

# Southwest Frittata

**Serves 2**

1/4 pound fresh chorizo sausage (available from specialty butchers), cut into 1-inch lengths
4 large eggs
1 tablespoon heavy cream
1 tablespoon unsalted butter
1 tablespoon finely chopped onion
1 boiled red Bliss potato, sliced 1/4-inch thick
1/2 cup shredded jack cheese
Salt and freshly ground black pepper
1 generous tablespoon sour cream
Crushed tortillas, for serving

Place a large sauté pan over medium-low heat. Add the chorizo and sauté gently, turning occasionally, for 12 to 15 minutes, or until done through.

Preheat the oven to 350°. In a bowl, beat the eggs with the cream.

In a 6-inch non-stick skillet, warm the butter over low heat. Add the onions and cook for 1 minute. Add the egg-cream mixture to the pan. Move the eggs around in the pan gently with a heat-resistant spatula (push the cooked eggs towards the center of the pan while tilting the pan; let the uncooked eggs fill in the empty space). Continue until the frittata is almost cooked through.

Just before the frittata will be done, arrange the potatoes, cooked chorizo, and jack cheese on top.

Season with salt and pepper. Place the pan in the oven for 2 minutes, or until the cheese has melted.

Remove from the oven and slide onto a heat-resistant plate. Serve with a heaping tablespoon of sour cream and crushed tortillas.

The key to good chicken salad is to poach the chicken at a low temperature in seasoned water. The water should be barely simmering – at most a heavy steam should be coming off the surface. You then want to remove the chicken from the water the moment it is cooked through. The resulting cooked chicken is tender, moist and flavorful.

*– Nick*

# Pesto Chicken Salad Sandwiches

### Serves 6

1 1/4 pounds boneless chicken breasts
Salt and freshly ground black pepper
3/4 cup mayonnaise
1/4 cup onion, finely chopped
1/4 cup celery, finely chopped
4 fresh basil leaves, finely chopped
1/4 cup good quality pesto (available at specialty stores)
1 1/2 lemons

**To serve:**
6 Kaiser rolls
Mayonnaise, as needed
Sliced iceberg or other crisp lettuce
Sliced tomato

In a medium saucepan, bring about 1 1/2 quarts of water to a boil and add 1/2 teaspoon of salt. Add the chicken breasts and immediately reduce the heat so the water is just barely simmering. Cook the chicken for 20 minutes, until firm and opaque through to the center. Remove the chicken from the cooking water and cool completely; cut into 1/2-inch cubes.

In a bowl, combine the chicken, mayonnaise, onion, celery, basil and pesto. Squeeze the lemons and add their juice to the salad.

Season with about 1 teaspoon of salt and 1/2 teaspoon of pepper. Mix well, taste, and adjust seasoning if necessary.

To serve, spread a little mayonnaise on each cut side of a Kaiser roll and mound the bottom half with chicken salad, lettuce, and tomato. Cover with the top of the roll.

# Tarragon Biscuits, Maple Syrup Ham, and Grainy Mustard Sauce

**Serves 4**

1 tablespoon vegetable oil
4 thin slices good quality ham, cut into 1/2-inch strips
2 tablespoons maple syrup
4 small, dressed green salads
Warm Tarrgon Biscuits (recipe follows), for serving
Grainy Mustard Sauce (see page 162), for serving

Make the biscuits, mustard sauce, and assemble the salads.

Place a sauté pan over high heat and add the oil. When it is hot, add the strips of ham and sauté just to warm them through. Add the maple syrup and cook for 1 minute, stirring.

Arrange the biscuits, dressed salads, and warm maple ham on the plates. Drizzle with the grainy mustard sauce, and serve at once.

One essential element to a good biscuit is eating them the moment they come out of the oven. They are tender little fluffballs, begging for butter, or in the case of this recipe, salty and sweet ham. Add a little grainy mustard sauce and you have yourself a yummy Southern appetizer.

*— Nick*

# Tarragon Biscuits

### Yield: 10 small biscuits

1 1/3 cups pastry flour
1/2 cup cake flour
1 tablespoon baking powder
1/4 teaspoon baking soda
1 teaspoon salt
1 1/2 teaspoons sugar
4 ounces (1 stick) cold unsalted butter, cut into small pieces
3/4 cup buttermilk, very cold
2 teaspoons finely chopped fresh tarragon leaves
Flour as needed for dusting
1/4 cup unsalted butter, melted, for brushing the biscuits

Preheat the oven to 375° and place a sheet of baking parchment on a large baking sheet. Into a large bowl, sift the pastry flour, cake flour, baking powder, baking soda, salt and sugar. Toss together, then add the cold butter bits and work with (clean) hands into pea-sized pieces (work quickly and with a light hand so the butter does not melt). As quickly as possible, mix in the cold buttermilk and tarragon, mixing just until blended.

Dust a clean surface with a little flour and scrape the dough out of the bowl onto the surface. Gently roll out the dough about 1-inch thick. With a 2-inch biscuit cutter, cut out as many rounds as possible, then reshape the remaining dough, roll out, and cut a few more biscuits. Brush with about half of the melted butter and bake for 12 to 15 minutes, until light golden brown. Brush with the remaining butter and serve.

(These are best when eaten right out of the oven! Having said that, any leftover biscuits may be reheated, wrapped in foil and warmed in a low oven, then consumed with butter and jam the following day.)

Make your own garlic oil as follows: Smash 4 peeled cloves of garlic with the side of a large, heavy knife. In a small saucepan, combine the garlic with 3/4 cup olive oil and warm until barely sizzling. Simmer until the garlic is pale golden, then remove from the heat and let cool. Strain out the garlic and use as desired.

*– Nick*

# Wild Mushroom Pizza with Caramelized Onions, Fontina, and Rosemary

From Chef Michael Tuohy, Woodfire Grill
Serves 2 to 4; makes two 8-inch pizzas

3 tablespoons unsalted butter, divided
1 tablespoon plus 1 teaspoon grapeseed oil
1 large onion, halved lengthwise, then thinly sliced crosswise (about 2 cups)
Salt and freshly ground black pepper

3/4 pound assorted wild mushrooms, such as cremini, oyster, chanterelle, and stemmed shiitake, cleaned and cut into bite-size pieces
3 to 4 garlic cloves, smashed with the side of a large, heavy knife
1 medium shallot, very finely chopped
Salt and freshly ground black pepper
3/4 cup dry white wine
1 teaspoon finely chopped fresh rosemary

1 pound pizza dough, at room temperature (available in many supermarkets and at friendly bakeries)
Cornmeal (for dusting)
Garlic oil, for brushing dough (available at specialty markets, or see note above)
1 cup grated fontina cheese

In a large, heavy skillet, combine 1 tablespoon of the butter with 1 tablespoon of the grapeseed oil and place over medium heat. Add the onion and sauté until very soft and slightly golden, stirring occasionally, about 25 minutes. Reduce the heat to very low and sizzle gently for 15 minutes more, until deep golden brown and caramelized. Season with 1/4 teaspoon salt and pepper to taste.

Place another large, heavy skillet over medium-high heat and in it, melt the remaining 2 tablespoons of butter with the remaining teaspoon of grapeseed oil. Add the mushrooms,

garlic, and shallot and sauté, stirring, for 4 minutes. Add the wine and simmer, stirring frequently until almost all the liquid has evaporated, about 10 minutes. Stir in the rosemary and season with $1/2$ teaspoon salt and $1/4$ teaspoon pepper, or to taste.

Preheat the oven to 500° at least 30 minutes before baking.

Position a rack in the bottom third of the oven and remove any other racks, to provide maximum maneuvering space. Place a heavy 17 x 11-inch baking sheet on the rack (invert, if it has a rim).

Divide the dough into 2 equal pieces and roll each one out on a lightly floured surface to an 8-inch round; allow the dough to rest for a few minutes if it springs back. Sprinkle another rimless baking sheet (or invert it, if rimmed) with cornmeal (to stop the dough from sticking). Transfer 1 dough round to the second baking sheet. Immediately brush the dough round lightly with garlic oil and sprinkle with $1/2$ cup of the cheese. Working quickly, scatter half the onions over the cheese, and scatter half the mushrooms over the onions. Sprinkle with salt.

Position the baking sheet holding the pizza at the far edge of 1 side of hot baking sheet that is in the oven. Tilt the pan holding the pizza and pull it back slowly, allowing the pizza to slide out onto the hot sheet. Bake for 6 minutes while you assemble the other pizza in the same way.

After 6 minutes, turn the first pizza around one half turn, and slide the other pizza onto the other end of the hot baking sheet, if there is room. Continue baking the first pizza for about 6 minutes more, or until the crust is deep brown. Turn the second pizza around and. using a large spatula, carefully transfer pizza to a cutting board. Let rest 1 minute, then slice into wedges and serve immediately. (Make the remaining pizza in the same way if it would not fit onto the baking sheet.)

# Soups & Salads

# Smoked Chicken Tomato Soup

**Serves 4**

4 ounces (1 stick) unsalted butter

1/2 onion, finely chopped

6 tablespoons all-purpose flour

1 1/4 quarts homemade chicken stock
or canned low-sodium broth

10-ounce can peeled tomatoes, with
all their juices, cut into 1/4-inch strips

1/2 roasted chicken, meat pulled from the bones,
and shredded

1 smoked Cornish game hen, meat pulled from
the bones, and shredded

1/2 cup heavy cream

6 fresh basil leaves, roughly chopped

6 fresh tarragon leaves, roughly chopped

Small croutons, homemade or store-bought, for serving

4 to 6 fresh basil leaves, cut finely, crosswise,
into chiffonade, for garnish

Place a large soup pot over medium heat and add the butter. Add the onions and cook gently, stirring occasionally, until tender, about 5 minutes. Stir in the flour and keep stirring until a smooth paste is formed. Slowly add the chicken stock, whisking all the time to avoid lumps. Continue whisking over medium heat until the liquid thickens. Add the tomato strips and cook for 20 minutes at a slow simmer. Stir in the pulled chicken and game hen, cream, and chopped herbs. Return to a simmer and serve in shallow bowls, garnishing each one with a few croutons and a little of the basil chiffonade.

My wife and I were on vacation in Venice and several restaurants served a wonderful and simple salad of arugula, cherry tomatoes and shredded raw cabbage. I loved the salad so much that I adapted it for Murphy's by adding young goat cheese and an emulsified arugula dressing.

*— Nick*

# Arugula, Goat Cheese, and Cherry Tomato Salad

### Serves 4

4 cups (about 4 ounces) baby arugula leaves, washed and dried thoroughly
4 cups (about 4 ounces) mesclun leaves, washed and dried if necessary
1/8 small head red cabbage, cored and very thinly sliced
1/2 pint cherry tomatoes, washed and halved
2 tablespoons balsamic vinegar
2 tablespoons extra-virgin olive oil
Sea salt and freshly ground black pepper
8 ounces soft, young goat cheese such as Montrachet, crumbled
Arugula Dressing (recipe follows)

In a large bowl, combine the arugula, mesclun, cabbage, and tomatoes. Toss together gently, then add the balsamic vinegar and olive oil. Season to taste with salt and pepper and toss again until thoroughly combined.

Divide the salad among four plates, then top each with an equal amount of the crumbled goat cheese. Drizzle with the dressing and serve at once.

## Arugula Dressing

### Yield: 1 cup

1 tablespoon white wine vinegar
Juice of 1 lemon (about 3 tablespoons)
2 tablespoons water
3/4 cup mayonnaise
2 tablespoons extra-virgin olive oil
1/2 fistful arugula leaves, washed and dried
4 leaves fresh tarragon
Sea salt and cayenne pepper

In a blender, combine the vinegar, lemon juice, water, and mayonnaise and blend until smooth, about 5 seconds. With the blender running, drizzle in the olive oil, then throw in the arugula and tarragon and season to taste with salt and cayenne. Refrigerate for up to 2 hours.

This is a soup my mother used to make for me when I was a child, and I remember loving it. When I discovered a newfound appreciation for all foods "Southern" (dumplings, fresh tomatoes, etc), I rejuvenated the soup for the restaurant.
Note: Make the soup first, then make the dumplings.

*– Nick*

# Creamy Tomato Soup with Dumplings

### Serves 6

2 tablespoons olive oil
1 medium onion, cut into 1-inch chunks
1/2 cup peeled garlic cloves, pushed through a press
1 (16-ounce) can whole peeled plum tomatoes, crushed
1 quart chicken stock, preferably homemade
Pinch of sugar
2 tablespoons grated Parmesan
1/2 cup heavy cream
6 leaves fresh basil, julienned (finely slivered crosswise)
1 1/2 teaspoons salt
1/2 teaspoon freshly ground black pepper

## For the Dumplings

2 cups bread flour
1/4 teaspoon baking soda
3/4 teaspoon baking powder
1 teaspoon salt
1/4 teaspoon pepper
6 tablespoons (3 ounces) cold unsalted butter, cut into small cubes
1 large egg, cold
1/2 cup cold buttermilk
Flour, for dusting work surface
Equipment: large vegetable steamer with a lid

In a large saucepan, warm the olive oil over medium heat. Add the onions and garlic and sweat until they begin to color slightly, about 8 minutes. Add the tomato, chicken stock, and sugar, bring up to a gentle simmer and cook for 20 minutes. Stir in the Parmesan and the cream and bring back to a boil. Remove from the heat and cool for 5 minutes, then puree in a blender or food processor until smooth. Stir in the basil, salt, and pepper. Set aside while you make the dumplings, below.

To serve, warm the soup, if necessary, and serve in wide shallow bowls with a few dumplings floating on top.

Bring about 2 inches of water to a simmer in the base of the steamer.

Into a large bowl, sift the flour, baking powder, baking soda, salt, and pepper. Add the butter pieces and work together with your fingertips until the butter is the size of small peas. In a small bowl, whisk together the egg and cold buttermilk. Add the buttermilk mixture to the flour mixture and blend together quickly with a fork, just until it begins to form a rough lump.

Bring the soft dough together into a mass and roll out on a lightly floured surface about 1/4-inch thick. Cut into 1- x 2-inch strips. Steam for about 10 minutes, or until cooked through.

# Panzanella, Tuscan Tomato and Bread Salad

From Chef Shaun Doty, Table 1280

Serves 6

3 pounds ripe heirloom tomatoes, carefully peeled, seeded, and quartered

1 cucumber, peeled and cut into 1/2-inch dice

1/2 cup shallots, very finely chopped (about 4 large shallots)

2 1/2 cups 1/2-inch cubes of stale French bread (remove crusts before cubing)

18 fresh basil leaves, torn into 1/2-inch pieces

1/4 cup extra-virgin olive oil

3 tablespoons red wine vinegar

8 anchovy filets, very finely chopped

Salt and freshly ground black pepper to taste

Chill six salad plates.

In a large bowl, combine the tomatoes, cucumber, shallots, bread, basil, olive oil, vinegar, and anchovies. Toss together gently and add salt and pepper to taste.

Divide the salad among the chilled plates and serve immediately.

# Fava Beans and Pecorino Toscano

From Chef Shaun Doty, Table 1280

Serves 6 as an appetizer

4 pounds fava beans, still in their pods

2 large shallots, minced

2 medium plum tomatoes, peeled, seeded, and finely diced

20 mint leaves, minced

1 cup diced pecorino Toscano

1/4 cup extra-virgin olive oil

3 tablespoons good quality red wine vinegar

Salt and freshly ground black pepper

Chill 6 small plates.

To prepare the fava beans, first remove them from their pods and discard the pods. Bring a generous amount of salted water to a boil in a large saucepan. Blanch the beans for 3 minutes, drain in a colander and stop the cooking by running under cold running water. When cool enough to handle, peel off and discard the thin whitish membrane from each bean. In a bowl, combine the shelled fava beans, shallots, tomatoes, mint, diced pecorino, olive oil, and red wine vinegar. Toss gently and season to taste with salt and pepper (the pecorino is quite salty).

Divide among the chilled plates and serve immediately.

If desired, warm the bowls in the oven before serving the soup. Another nice touch is to lightly dust the rim of each warm bowl with fennel pollen, for an extra aromatic boost.

# Fennel Soup with Nasturtiums and Fennel Pollen

From Chef Michael Tuohy, Woodfire Grill
Serves 6 to 8

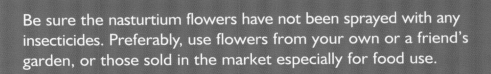

1/2 cup grapeseed oil
3 bulbs fennel, trimmed and coarsely chopped
1 onion, coarsely chopped
1 leek, well washed and coarsely chopped
1 rib celery, coarsely chopped
4 cloves garlic, coarsely chopped
1 cup white wine
2 quarts vegetable stock or water

Half an Idaho potato, coarsely chopped
2 tablespoons fennel pollen
1 cup white balsamic vinegar
1 cup heavy cream (optional)
Kosher salt and freshly ground white pepper
Best quality extra-virgin olive oil, for garnish
Nasturtium flowers (very fresh), for garnish

In a large saucepan, warm the grapeseed oil over medium-low heat. Add the fennel, onion, leek, celery, and garlic; add a little salt, and stir to coat with the oil. Cook until softened and translucent, about 10 minutes. Add the white wine and, when it has almost all evaporated, add the stock, potato, and fennel pollen. Bring to a simmer and cook, partially covered, for 30 minutes.

Stir in the white balsamic vinegar, heavy cream (if using), and salt white pepper to taste. Using an immersion blender, puree until smooth (or transfer to a blender and puree).

Ladle 6 to 8 ounces of soup into each bowl and drizzle with a little extra-virgin olive oil. Place a few nasturtium flowers on the surface of the soup and serve immediately. These are available in good markets and specialty food stores and on web sites.

Be sure the nasturtium flowers have not been sprayed with any insecticides. Preferably, use flowers from your own or a friend's garden, or those sold in the market especially for food use.

# Lobster Noodle Soup

From Gerry Klaskala, Aria
Serves 8

1 cup Borlotti (cranberry) beans

4 live lobsters, about 1 1/4 pounds each

4 tablespoons olive oil

Salt and freshly ground black pepper

Half a large onion, cut into 1/2-inch dice

4 stalks of celery, cut into 1/2-inch dice

3 large leeks, white parts only, well washed and cut into 1/2-inch dice

2 carrots, peeled and cut into 1/2-inch dice

4 cloves garlic, minced

Two 16-ounce cans plum tomatoes, with their juices, roughly chopped

1 cup dry white wine

Coarsely chopped leaves from 1/2 bunch fresh thyme

2 teaspoons finely chopped fresh tarragon, leaves only

8 cups light chicken or seafood stock, preferably homemade

2 bunches Swiss chard, both stems and leaves, finely chopped

Leaves from 1/2 bunch Italian (flat-leaf) parsley, coarsely chopped

1/2 pound bow-tie pasta

The night before: Soak the beans in 3 cups of water, overnight.

In the morning, drain the beans and cover them with 2 1/2 times their volume of water. Bring to a simmer and cook until tender, about 3 hours. Drain.

Brush the lobsters on all sides with about 2 tablespoons of the olive oil, and season with salt. Place a large heavy skillet over medium-high heat and add the remaining 2 tablespoons of oil. When it is very hot, place in the lobsters curved side down and cook until deep pinky-orange from head to tail, 5 to 6 minutes. Turn the lobsters over and cook for about 30 seconds more, until uniformly orange. Remove from the heat. When cool enough to handle, split the lobsters and remove the digestive sacs. Remove all the meat from the lobsters. Cut into half-inch dice, cover, and set aside. Return the lobster bodies to the pan and return the pan to medium heat.

Add the onions and cook for 3 minutes, stirring. Add the celery and carrots and cook for 3 more minutes. Add the leeks and cook for an additional minute. Stir in the garlic and cook for 30 seconds. Add the tomatoes, thyme, and tarragon, cook for 4 minutes, then add the white wine and cook for 3 minutes.

Add the stock and bring to a simmer. Cook gently for 45 minutes. With a slotted spoon, remove the lobster shells, then add the Swiss chard and cook until tender, about 15 minutes. Add the cooked borlotti beans and the parsley, and adjust the seasoning with salt and pepper.

Cook the bow-tie pasta until al dente and divide among warmed soup bowls. Add the lobster meat and ladle the hot "minestrone" over the top. Serve immediately.

# Sausage, Bean, and Winter Vegetable Soup

Serves 6

1/2 pound bulk, spicy pork sausage
About 1/4 of a head of napa cabbage, chopped
2 slices raw bacon, finely chopped
1/2 onion, coarsely chopped
1 stalk celery, coarsely chopped
1 small carrot, peeled and coarsely chopped
1 1/2 quarts chicken stock, preferably homemade

1 Russet potato, peeled and coarsely chopped
4 cloves garlic, smashed with the side of a large heavy knife
Salt and freshly ground black pepper
1/2 cup canned, cooked beans, drained (such as navy, pinto, kidney beans, etc.)
Grated Swiss cheese, for garnish

Preheat the oven to 350°. Spread the sausage meat evenly on a rimmed baking sheet and cook for 15 minutes, or until cooked through with no trace of pink remaining. Cool, then crumble into teaspoon-sized pieces and set aside

Place a large, heavy soup pot over medium-low heat and add the bacon and the cabbage. Cook gently, stirring occasionally, until the bacon has rendered its fat and the cabbage is tender, 20 to 25 minutes.

Add the onion, celery, carrot, chicken stock, potato, and garlic. Season with 1/2 tablespoon salt and about 1/4 teaspoon pepper. Increase the heat and bring to a simmer; reduce heat and cook gently until all the vegetables are tender, about 30 minutes. Stir the cooked sausage and drained beans into the soup, taste for seasoning, and return to a simmer. To serve, ladle into soup bowls and scatter each with some grated Swiss cheese.

One of the nifty tricks I learned: When making a soup with sausage, cook the sausage separately from the soup, drain off the fat, and then crumble or cut the sausage and add it to the soup. Why? 1. It removes all the fat that would otherwise be in the soup, and 2. the sausage doesn't taste washed-out like it tends to when you cook it in the soup.

I was invited to prepare a dish at the Virginia-Highland Greenmarket using locally grown zucchini; this is the recipe born of that event. Vegetable soups are a bit tricky in that they tend to be somewhat tasteless unless you handle the vegetables properly. It is important to sweat them, to excise all their liquid before adding the stock. I always tell my prep staff, "You can always add more liquid to the soup but it is really hard to remove it."

*– Nick*

# Spicy Puree of Zucchini and Basil Soup

**Serves 4 to 6**

1 tablespoon unsalted butter
3 medium zucchini, thinly sliced
2 cloves garlic, pressed or very finely chopped
2 tablespoons very finely chopped onion
1 quart homemade chicken stock or canned low-sodium broth
1 1/2 pinches hot pepper flakes
3/4 cup heavy cream
10 large leaves of basil
1 teaspoon salt
4 tablespoons fresh sheep's milk ricotta cheese
  (full-fat ricotta may be substituted)
Sprigs of bush basil or opal basil, for garnish
Best quality extra-virgin olive oil, for drizzling

Place a large, heavy soup pot over low heat and add the butter. When it has foamed, add the zucchini, garlic, and onion and cook, stirring occasionally, until tender, about 5 minutes. Add the chicken stock and pepper flakes and increase the heat to high. Simmer until the zucchini is very tender, about 20 minutes. Stir in the cream and basil leaves, and return the soup to a boil. Remove from the heat and let stand for 5 minutes. Holding the top down firmly with a folded dish towel, puree the soup in a blender until it is very smooth. Ladle into soup bowls and place a tablespoon of the ricotta in each bowl. Garnish with a sprig of bush or opal basil, and drizzle a little extra-virgin olive oil over the top.

# Slow-Roasted Vidalia Onion Soup

From Chef Michael Tuohy, Woodfire Grill
Serves 12

6 medium Vidalia onions, papery outer layers removed
Olive oil, for roasting the onions
Kosher salt and ground white pepper
1/4 cup canola or grapeseed oil
2 leeks, white part only, well washed and finely chopped
2 ribs celery, finely chopped
2 quarts homemade chicken stock or canned, low-sodium broth
1 cup sweet sherry
1 cup heavy cream
2 tablespoons finely chopped fresh thyme leaves
1 bunch fresh chives, for garnish

Preheat the oven to 300°. Place each onion separately in a square of aluminum foil and add a few drops of olive oil and a pinch each of salt and white pepper. Wrap well and place in the hot oven until the onions feel tender all the way through, about 1 1/2 hours (or, you could roast the onions in the coals of a fireplace or a grill pit).

Place a large soup pot over medium-low heat and add the oil. When it is warm, add the leeks and celery; cook until softened but not browned, stirring occasionally for about 7 minutes. Add the chicken stock and sherry and bring to a simmer. Remove onions from their foil, quarter and add them to the pot. Cook, stirring occasionally, for about 45 minutes, until the onions are very soft and translucent. Stir in the cream and thyme and remove from heat.

In a blender, while holding the top on securely with a folded dish towel, puree the soup in batches until smooth. Add and blend in about 1 teaspoon salt and 1/4 teaspoon white pepper, or to taste. Ladle into soup bowls. With scissors, snip a generous amount of chives over the top of each bowl, and serve at once.

# Appetizers

When I was a student in Paris in 1989 I used to frequent a small restaurant behind the Pantheon that served a wonderful salad of goat cheese, greens, oranges, and apples.

*– Nick*

# Orange and Goat Cheese Salad with Citrus Vinaigrette

**Serves 6**

2 small beets
Olive or vegetable oil, for roasting the beets
2 oranges
1 apple, washed
12 cups loosely packed mixed greens
$1/2$ cup Citrus Vinaigrette (recipe follows, stir well before drizzling)
Salt and freshly ground black pepper
8 ounces semi-soft goat cheese such as Montrachet, crumbled
$1/2$ cup pine nuts, lightly toasted

Preheat the oven to 350°. Wash the beets and rub them all over with a little oil. Place in a small roasting pan and roast until tender, about 1 $1/2$ hours. Cool and peel the beets, slice them $1/4$-inch thick, and set aside.

Peel the oranges with a small, sharp knife to remove all the pith, then cut down close to each membrane on either side of each segment to release the "supremes." Remove all seeds. Quarter and core the apple and then further slice the quarters $1/4$-inch thick.

In a bowl, combine and gently toss together the orange, apple, and mixed greens. Drizzle with just enough of the vinaigrette to lightly coat the greens (reserve remaining dressing for the beets).

Toss the salad gently and season to taste with salt and pepper.

Flash forward to the present: One day, Chuck Taylor whipped up a delicious citrus vinaigrette, and I fondly recalled that salad from my past. I combined the two, added pine nuts and roasted beets, and came up with what I think is a refreshing and interesting winter salad. Blood oranges, when available, are a pretty addition.
PS: I love this vinaigrette so much that when we have it around, I put it on everything!

Divide among six plates. In the same bowl, toss the beets with some of the remaining vinaigrette and a little salt and pepper, just to coat evenly (reserve any remaining vinaigrette for another use.) Divide the beets among the salads, placing them on top of the greens. Sprinkle each with some of the crumbled goat cheese and toasted pine nuts, and serve at once.

## Citrus Vinaigrette

**Yield: About 2 1/2 cups**

1 orange
1 lemon
1 lime
1 cup extra-virgin olive oil
Additional 1/2 cup orange juice, preferably fresh
1/4 cup red wine vinegar
Pinch of salt and freshly ground black pepper
2 tablespoons granulated sugar

Wash and dry all the citrus fruits, then remove their zests with a zester (or use a vegetable peeler, making sure to leave all the white pith behind, then finely chop the strips of zest). Juice the fruits into a bowl, add all the zest, and the olive oil, orange juice, red wine vinegar, salt and pepper to taste, and the sugar. Whisk until smooth and taste for seasoning. Re-whisk just before serving.

There are several options for serving this gravlax-like salmon, which should be sliced as thinly as possible with a long, sharp knife.

# Citrus-Cured Salmon

From Chef Michael Tuohy, Woodfire Grill
Serves 8 to 10 as an appetizer

- 12-ounce side of fresh salmon, skin on, pin bones removed
- 1 cup Kosher salt
- 1 cup granulated sugar
- Zest and juice from half a lemon
- Zest and juice from half an orange
- Zest and juice from half a lime
- 1 tablespoon coriander seeds
- 1 tablespoon fennel seeds

Pat the salmon dry with paper towels. Place, skin side down, on a large sheet of plastic wrap. In a small bowl, combine and mix together the salt, sugar, citrus zests and juices, coriander seeds, and fennel seeds. Spread this moist, paste-like mixture over the flesh of the salmon filet, covering it completely. Place another sheet of plastic wrap on the top and tuck in the sides, then bring up the bottom plastic to seal the package securely. Place between two baking sheets and weigh down the top pan with a couple of heavy cans. Place in the refrigerator and let cure for 18 to 24 hours. Remove from refrigerator, unwrap, and rinse in cold water to remove the cure mixture. Pat dry thoroughly with paper towels and rewrap tightly in fresh plastic wrap until ready to slice and serve, up to three days.

1. Use as a garnish for your favorite potato cake or rösti, then top with sour cream and caviar (or capers), and scatter with chives
2. Use as a topping for green salad
3. Mound a slice or two on a rectangle of rye or pumpernickel bread and serve with pots of crème fraiche or sour cream, chopped hard-boiled eggs, salmon roe caviar, and/or other varieties of caviar.

I knew that I wanted to serve this dish, so I went to my most excellent lead line cook, Chael Pinto (who is Mexican), and asked him to come up with an authentic recipe for a tequila-lime base for cooking mussels.

*– Nick*

# Mussels with Tequila-Lime Sauce

Serves 4

1 tablespoon unsalted butter

1 jalapeño chile, stemmed, seeds removed, and finely minced

1 onion, cut into 1/2-inch dice (about 2 cups)

2 scallions, white and light green parts, finely chopped

1/4 cup chicken stock, preferably homemade (or substitute vegetable stock, for a vegetarian dish)

1/4 cup good quality tequila

1 cup heavy cream

Juice of 2 fresh limes

1 teaspoon salt and 1/4 freshly ground black pepper, or to taste

4 quarts live mussels, preferably from Prince Edward Island, well rinsed and beards pulled off

Leaves only, from 1/4 bunch of cilantro, washed, dried, and cut into chiffonade (slivered)

Crusty bread, for serving (optional)

In a large, heavy pot, combine everything except the mussels, cilantro, and bread. Simmer for 10 minutes, partially covered.

Add the mussels and cook, covered, until all the mussels have opened, about 5 minutes (discard any mussels which have not opened after 7 minutes). Shake the pan gently every now and then to redistribute the mussels. Ladle the mussels, with a little of their liquid, into large shallow bowls and scatter a generous amount of cilantro over the top of each. Serve at once.

If desired, serve with crusty bread, for sopping up the delicious juices.

When preparing mussels in a professional kitchen, you always make a large batch of highly alcoholic and strongly flavored base to which you later add the mussels and other flavoring ingredients. The resulting liquid is really tasty and well balanced.

Cremini mushrooms are young portobello mushrooms and are noted for their rich texture and meaty flavor.

# Cremini Mushroom Dip

From Hector Santiago, Pura Vida

Serves 10 to 12

1 pound cremini mushrooms cut into 1-inch cubes
2 tablespoons canola oil
1/4 red onion, finely chopped
2 teaspoons Spanish sherry vinegar
1/2 teaspoon salt

2 cloves garlic, minced
1/8 teaspoon freshly cracked black pepper
1 pint sour cream
1 tablespoons fineiy chopped parsley
1 teaspoon fineiy chopped thyme
1 tablespoon white truffle oil

onions
vinegar
salt
garlic
ail
mush rooms
pepper
etc

In a bowl, combine onions, vinegar and salt. Let pickle for 10 minutes. Add garlic mix well.

While onions are pickling, heat oil in a frying pan and sauté mushrooms until golden brown and cooked through, 6 to 8 minutes. Place mushrooms in a food processor and chop finely.

Place mushrooms in a bowl and add onion mixture. Mix well. Season with black pepper. Add sour cream parsley, tarragon and truffie oil Mix well. Adjust seasoning with salt, pepper, truffle oil and vinegar to taste.

Serve with yuca chips or other tropical root vegetable chips.

# Risi e Bisi

From Chef Shaun Doty, Table 1280

Serves 8 as an appetizer

2 cups English peas (about 5 pounds of peas in their shells)

1 1/2 quarts unsalted chicken broth

1/4 cup (1/4 stick) plus 2 tablespoons unsalted butter

2 cups Arborio or Carnaroli rice

1/4 cup very finely chopped shallots (about 2 shallots)

1/2 cup grated Reggiano-Parmigiano cheese

Salt and freshly ground pepper

Bring a generous amount of lightly salted water to a boil in a large pot. Add the shelled peas and blanch for 1 minute. Drain well and run under cold running water to stop the cooking. Take about 1/2 cup of the cooked peas and, while they are still warm, puree them in a mini-prep food processor (or a blender), until smooth. Set the pea puree and the blanched peas aside.

Place the chicken broth in a saucepan and warm to just below the simmering point. Keep warm.

Place a large, heavy pot over medium heat and add 1/4 cup of the butter. When the foam begins to subside, add the rice and shallots and sauté, stirring frequently, for 3 minutes.

Add the hot chicken broth in increments of approximately 1 cup. Stir continuously, until the rice absorbs the previous addition before adding another cup of hot broth. Keep stirring and adding broth until the rice reaches the desired "al dente" consistency, 10 to 15 minutes (The center of each kernel of rice should still have a bit of a "bite").

Remove the pan from the heat and stir in the peas, pea puree, grated cheese, and remaining 2 tablespoons butter. Season with 1 teaspoon salt and 1/4 teaspoon pepper, or to taste. Serve at once.

Make sure to buy "dry" scallops. You will probably need to call around in order to find them. Most scallops are pumped with sodium solution, which make them seem plump and moist. However, when you cook those same, seemingly-moist scallops, they release a lot of liquid, they don't brown properly and they taste funny.

*– Nick*

# Scallops with Carrot-Ginger Puree and Garlic Butter

**Serves 4**

2 pounds large, dry pack scallops
   (U10 count, i.e. 10 scallops per pound)
Salt and freshly ground black pepper
1 tablespoon vegetable oil
Garlic Butter (recipe follows), at room temperature, for serving
Carrot-Ginger Puree (recipe follows), warm, for serving

Make the garlic butter and carrot puree, if you have not already done so.

Place a large sauté pan over medium-high heat. Pat the scallops to be sure they are completely dry, and season both sides lightly with salt. When the oil is very hot, add and sauté the scallops for 2 to 3 minutes on each side, depending on their size.

Make a bed of the carrot puree on each plate and divide the hot scallops evenly, placing them on top of the puree. Smear each one with a dab of the garlic butter and serve immediately.

## Carrot-Ginger Puree:

1 pound carrots, peeled and cut into 1-inch lengths
$^1/_4$ cup vegetable oil
1 teaspoon grated ginger
1 $^1/_2$ teaspoons crushed garlic
$^1/_8$ teaspoon ground cayenne
1 tablespoon brown sugar
2 tablespoons unsalted butter, cut into 4 pieces
2 tablespoons whipping cream, or as needed

In a saucepan of generously salted boiling water, cook the carrots until tender but not mushy, about 20 minutes. Drain in a colander and place in a blender or food processor.

In a mini-prep food processor, puree the vegetable oil, ginger, garlic, and cayenne until smooth. Transfer this puree to a small saucepan and sauté for about 3 minutes, until golden and aromatic

Add the aromatic puree to the blender with the carrots. Add the brown sugar and cubed butter and blend until smooth. Add just enough of the cream to make a nice, smooth puree. Season with salt and pepper and keep warm in a double boiler over gently simmering water until serving time.

## Garlic Butter:

4 ounces (1 stick) unsalted butter, at room temperature
1 teaspoon crushed or minced garlic
1 teaspoon finely chopped red onion
$^1/_2$ teaspoon finely snipped chives
$^1/_4$ teaspoon finely chopped fresh tarragon
Splash of dry white wine
Juice of 1 lemon
2 pinches crushed red pepper
2 pinches salt

In a bowl, whisk together all the ingredients until evenly blended. Refrigerate, covered, if desired, but be sure to return to room temperature before smearing on the scallops.

"Dry" sea scallops, although more expensive than treated scallops, sear well and taste fresh and of the sea. Besides, when you buy treated scallops, you are essentially paying for water so there is no real savings.

# Papitas Bravas, with Colombian Avocado Aji

From Hector Santiago, Pura Vida

**Serves 4 as an appetizer**

1 pound tiny gold potatoes
Flesh from 2 ripe avocados
2 scallions, coarsely chopped
2 small green serrano chilis, stemmed, seeded and finely chopped
1 stalk celery, coarsely chopped
1/4 cup water

1/2 teaspoon salt
Juice of 1 lime
1/2 cup extra virgin olive oil
1/4 bunch cilantro, leaves only, finely chopped
2 teaspoons red onion, minced
Chili powder to taste
Vegetable oil as needed, for deep frying

Wash and dry potatoes.  Freeze overnight or longer.

For the avocado aji:

Place avocados, scallions, chilis, celery, water, salt and lime juice in a blender. Blend until smooth. Add olive oil slowly, while blending. Place in a bowl and add the cilantro and red onion. Mix well.

Adjust seasoning to taste and chill.

In a deep fryer or deep pot, add 5 inches of oil and heat to and fry frozen potatoes at 350° until crispy. Drain, and season with salt and chili powder. Serve topped with chilled avocado aji.

Note: Place the cipollini onions in a small pan, coat very lightly with olive oil and season, then roast alongside the potatoes for 35 to 45 minutes, tossing every 10 minutes or so, until golden brown.

# The Big Murphy

From Gerry Klaskala, served at Murphy's
Serves 4

4 large baking potatoes (14 to 16 ounces each)
2 tablespoons unsalted butter, melted
2 teaspoons Kosher salt, for baking the potatoes
12 small asparagus tips, about 2 inches long
3 ounces snow peas, blanched for
   25 seconds and shocked
1 ½ teaspoons olive oil
4 ounces fresh morel mushrooms,
   brushed clean and halved, if large

1 medium shallot, finely chopped
8 cipollini onions, roasted until golden and halved
   (or quartered if large; see Note above)
Kosher salt and freshly ground black pepper
1 tablespoon finely snipped chives
White truffle oil, for serving
Crème fraiche, for garnish
Additional snipped chives, for garnish

Preheat the oven to 375°. Wash and dry the potatoes, brush with melted butter, and season generously with the Kosher salt. Place the potatoes on a rack, then place the rack on a baking sheet. Bake for one hour and 15 minutes, until tender.

While the potatoes are cooking: Place a bowl of iced water near the stove. In a pan of salted, boiling water, immerse the asparagus tips. Blanch for 2 to 3 minutes, depending on their size, then retrieve with a slotted spoon and dump into the ice water. Repeat with the snow peas, blanching them for only 25 seconds. Remove from the water and place on paper towels.

Place a heavy sauté pan over medium heat and add the olive oil. Add and sauté the morels for 2 to 3 minutes, until aromatic and slightly crisped. Add the shallots and cook gently for 30 seconds more, but do not allow to brown. Add the asparagus, snow peas, and roasted onions. Cook for 2 to 3 minutes more, or until just heated through. Season with salt and pepper to taste, and stir in the chives.

As soon as the potatoes are done, use a sharp knife to make a slit in the top of each one. Using a towel to protect your fingers, pinch the potatoes to pop them open. Season the inside of the potatoes with kosher salt and freshly ground pepper. Drizzle the inside of each potato with a little white truffle oil.

Place the potatoes on individual serving plates and top with the vegetable mixture, dividing it evenly. Place a dollop of crème fraiche on each one, sprinkle with a few chives, and serve at once.

# Main Courses

# Italian Meatloaf with Marinara Sauce

Serves 6

Half a large onion, finely chopped
1 clove garlic, minced
1 cup completely thawed frozen spinach, very well-squeezed and chopped
2 pounds ground beef chuck
1/4 pound mild Italian sausage (use bulk sausage or remove the casings)
1/2 pound spicy Italian sausage (use bulk or remove the casings)
1 large egg
1/2 cup grated Parmesan

1/2 cup dry breadcrumbs
1/4 teaspoon salt
1/4 teaspoon freshly ground black pepper
Small pinch each, of: dried thyme, dried basil, dried oregano

To serve:
1 tablespoon vegetable oil
Marinara Sauce (recipe follows)
Chopped fresh basil and grated Parmesan, for garnish

The night before serving: Preheat the oven to 350°. In a large bowl, combine the onion, garlic, spinach, ground beef, both sausages, egg, Parmesan, breadcrumbs, salt, pepper, and herbs. Mix together, first with a long fork, and then with clean hands, until evenly combined.

Form into a loaf shape and place on a rimmed baking sheet. Cover the pan with foil and bake until just cooked through (it should measure 155° at the center), about 45 minutes.

Let cool to room temperature on the baking sheet, then refrigerate overnight.

To serve, cut the meatloaf into thick slices. Place a large skillet over medium heat and add the oil. Sauté the slices, in batches if necessary to avoid crowding the pan, until slightly browned on both sides, about 3 minutes on each side. Transfer to warmed plates and ladle some of the marinara sauce over each slice. Scatter with basil and Parmesan and serve at once.

# Marinara Sauce

### Yield: 1 cup

1 tablespoon olive oil
1 clove garlic, minced
Pinch of crushed red pepper
16-ounce can Italian plum tomatoes, drained,
and coarsely chopped
Pinch of dried basil
Pinch of dried oregano
Salt and freshly ground black pepper

Place a large saucepan over medium low heat and add the olive oil. Cook the garlic and red pepper, stirring frequently, until only just golden and aromatic (don't let the garlic scorch!). Add the tomatoes, basil, oregano, and 1/4 teaspoon each of salt and pepper. Bring up to a simmer and cook gently for 10 minutes. Pass through a moulis or a food mill, or purée in a blender or food processor.

# Grouper with Garlic Shrimp Sauce

Serves 4

4 large grouper filets, about 8 ounces each
1 tablespoon vegetable oil
Salt and freshly ground black pepper
6 ounces cleaned baby shrimp
Italian parsley
1 pound trimmed broccolini, well washed and
  chopped into large pieces (both stems and florets)
1 tablespoon extra-virgin olive oil
Garlic Shrimp Sauce, warm (recipe follows)

Place a large sauté pan over medium-high heat and add the oil.

Season both sides of the grouper filets with salt and pepper. When the oil is hot, sauté the filets for 2 to 3 minutes on one side, until lightly brown. Carefully turn the filets and add the baby shrimp to the pan. Cook for 2 to 3 minutes more, until the grouper is golden on both sides. Set the pan aside.

Place another pan over medium heat and add the olive oil. When it is hot, add the broccolini and sauté for 7 to 8 minutes, stirring occasionally, until crisp-tender. Season to taste with salt and pepper.

Place some of the broccolini on each plate and place a grouper filet on the top. Spoon over some of the sauce and serve at once.

## Garlic Shrimp Sauce

1 tablespoon unsalted butter
2 tablespoons minced garlic
2 tablespoons white wine
3 plum tomatoes, seeded and diced
1 1/4 cups chicken stock, preferably homemade
Pinch of granulated sugar, or as needed
Salt and freshly ground black pepper
1 tablespoon cornstarch whisked with
  2 tablespoons water

Place a sauté pan over medium-low heat and add the butter. Add the garlic and sweat until golden, stirring (don't let it scorch). Stir in the white wine and simmer until reduced by about half. Add the diced tomato and simmer for 5 minutes more, then add the chicken stock and simmer for 10 minutes. Season to taste with salt, pepper, and sugar. Increase the heat to high. When the sauce boils (whisking all the time), drizzle in the cornstarch mixture and keep whisking until thickened, 1 to 2 minutes. Remove from the heat. (The sauce may be warmed over low heat just before serving, if necessary.)

# Fresh Pasta with Rabbit and Porcini Ragout and Parmesan

From Chef Gerry Klaskala, Aria
Serves 6

1 ounce dried porcini mushrooms
1 tablespoon vegetable oil
1 whole fresh rabbit, meat cut from the bone and cut into 1/2-inch cubes, bones reserved
4 ribs celery, coarsely chopped
1 carrot, coarsely chopped
1 leek, well washed and coarsely chopped
2 whole cloves garlic
2 bay leaves

2 tablespoons olive oil
1 onion, finely chopped
1/2 cup finely chopped celery root (celeriac)
1 carrot, finely chopped
1 cup finely chopped Shitake mushrooms (remove stems before chopping)
3 garlic cloves, minced or pushed through a press
2 tablespoons tomato paste
1 bay leaf
1 cup dry white wine
Salt and freshly ground black pepper

**To serve:**
1 teaspoon Kosher salt
1 pound fresh pappardelle noodles
1 tablespoon unsalted butter
1/2 cup coarsely chopped flat-leaf (Italian) parsley leaves
1/2 cup freshly grated Reggiano Parmigiano

In a Pyrex jug, cover the porcini mushrooms with hot water and let stand for 1 hour. Remove and squeeze dry, reserving the liquid. Finely chop the mushrooms and set them and the liquid aside.

In a large saucepan, warm the vegetable oil over medium heat. Add the rabbit bones and lightly brown, stirring, for about 10 minutes. Add the celery, carrot, and leek and stir until lightly colored. Stir in the garlic cloves and bay leaves and cover with water

by about 1 inch. Bring to a simmer, partially cover the pan and cook for 2 $\frac{1}{2}$ hours. Strain and set aside, discarding the solids. (You should have about 3 cups.)

Place a large, heavy sauce-pan over medium heat and add the olive oil. When it is hot, add and lightly color the diced rabbit. Remove rabbit with a slotted spoon and set aside on a platter. Add the onion and cook for 3 minutes, stirring. Add the celery root and carrot, cook for 3 more minutes, then add the Shitake mushrooms and cook for four minutes. Add the garlic and cook for 30 seconds, then stir in the tomato paste and bay leaf, and cook for 4 minutes (don't let the tomato paste scorch). Stir in the white wine and cook for 4 minutes.

Add the browned rabbit, chopped porcini, and porcini-soaking liquid and cover with 2 cups of the rabbit stock. Bring to a slow simmer, partially cover the pan, and cook for 1 to 1 $\frac{1}{2}$ hours, or until the rabbit is tender. Adjust the seasonings with salt and pepper.

To serve: Bring a large pot of water to a boil and add the Kosher salt. Add the pasta and cook for a minute or two, until al dente. Drain the pasta. Ladle half the rabbit ragout into a large metal bowl. Add the butter, parsley, and Reggiano Parmigiano. Add the hot pasta and toss together evenly. Serve in warmed bowls topped with the remaining rabbit ragout, passing additional Reggiano Parmigiano on the side.

# Fried Grouper with Poached Eggs and Hollandaise

Serves 4

4 thin, skinless filets of grouper, about 4 ounces each
Salt and freshly ground black pepper
3 large eggs, for the egg wash
1 cup all-purpose flour seasoned with salt and pepper
2 cups dry breadcrumbs
1/2 cup vegetable oil
1 teaspoon white vinegar
6 extra large eggs, for poaching
1 large, ripe tomato, sliced
Freshly made, warm Hollandaise, for serving (recipe follows)
Snipped chives, for garnish

Season both sides of the fish filets with salt and pepper. Place the eggs in a shallow bowl, whisk until smooth, and season with salt and pepper. Place the flour in another shallow bowl and season with salt and pepper. Place the breadcrumbs in a third bowl.

Dredge each piece of fish first in the flour, shaking off the excess. Then dip into the beaten eggs, coating both sides. Dredge through the breadcrumbs.

Place a large skillet over medium heat and add the oil. When it is hot, fry the fish until golden, about 3 minutes on each side, turning over carefully. Drain on paper towels and keep warm in a low oven until ready to serve.

Add enough water to a large sauté pan or skillet to come 1 1/2 inches up the sides. Add the vinegar and bring just to a simmer. Break 1 egg into a small cup and slide gently into the water. Repeat with remaining eggs, keeping them as far apart as possible. Poach at a bare simmer until the whites are

I like the juxtaposition of the crunchy fried briny food (grouper) with the fatty, rich neutral food (egg yolk).

firm but the yolks are still runny, 2 to 3 minutes. Remove with a slotted spoon and drain briefly on paper towels.

To serve, layer a piece of fried grouper, some of the tomato, and a poached egg on each plate. Nap with the hollandaise, scatter with chives, and serve immediately.

## Hollandaise

2 tablespoons white wine vinegar

3 tablespoons cold water

$^{1}/_{4}$ teaspoon salt

8 ounces (2 sticks) unsalted butter, cut into
small pieces and softened to room temperature

3 large egg yolks

1 teaspoon fresh lemon juice

Pinch of cayenne pepper

In a heavy saucepan, combine the vinegar, water, and salt. Place over high heat and boil until reduced to 3 tablespoons, about 4 minutes. Let cool for 5 minutes while you melt the butter.

In another small saucepan, warm the butter only until melted.

Add the yolks to the vinegar mixture and use a flexible whisk to whisk the mixture over very low heat until smooth, slightly thickened, and mousse-like, just a minute or two. Use a heat-cheater if your stove can't be adjusted to very low heat, and be careful not to scramble the yolks! Whisk in the warm butter 1 tablespoon at a time, lifting the pan occasionally to stop the sauce from getting too hot (in which case it will separate).

Add each piece of butter as previous one is absorbed. Remove from the heat and whisk in the lemon juice, cayenne, and salt to taste. Serve within ten minutes of finishing the sauce, or keep warm in a thermos bottle. (It can not be reheated, or it will separate.)

# Murphy's Best Pasta Sauce

From Mike Hufler

Makes 5 Cups, serves 8 to 12

6 tablespoons unsalted butter

1/2 cup finely chopped sweet onions

3 cloves garlic, minced

1/4 cup all-purpose flour

1 1/2 cups low-sodium chicken broth or homemade stock

2 tablespoons chicken stock base (available in well-stocked markets), or 2 bouillon cubes

3 cups heavy cream

2 tablespoons finely chopped fresh tarragon

1/4 cup finely chopped fresh basil

1 tablespoon finely chopped fresh mint

1 tablespoon kosher salt

1/4 teaspoon white pepper, preferably freshly ground

1/4 cup fresh lemon juice

**To serve, per person:**

6 ounces cooked pasta of your choice

4 ounces grilled shrimp or chicken

1/2 cup Murphy's Best Pasta Sauce, hot

In a large, heavy saucepan, melt the butter over medium-low heat. Add the onions and garlic and cook, stirring frequently, until softened and translucent, about 5 minutes. Stir in the flour until the mixture forms a paste. Reduce the heat to very low and cook, stirring frequently for about 5 minutes to cook off the raw taste of the flour. Slowly add the broth or stock and the chicken base, whisking constantly to blend it evenly with the roux. Bring the mixture to a boil, reduce the heat to a simmer, and cook for 5 minutes. Stir in the heavy cream, return to a simmer, and cook for 5 minutes more. Remove the pan from the heat and stir in the tarragon, basil, mint, salt, and pepper. Stir in the lemon juice and taste for seasoning. Adjust with salt, pepper, or lemon juice as desired.

To serve, depending on the number of diners, combine half the sauce with the pasta of your choice in a warmed bowl. Add grilled shrimp or sliced, grilled chicken, and top with the remaining, deliciously rich sauce.

I knew that I wanted to serve a Tuna Niçoise, but I wanted something a little out of the ordinary. I took the basic flavors and ingredients from the Nice region – olives, tomatoes, fennel, etc. – and tweaked them a little, to come up with this dish. The fennel confit would also make a tasty vegetarian appetizer with grilled farm bread.

*– Nick*

# Tuna Niçoise

### Serves 4

**For the tapenade vinaigrette:**
- 1 clove garlic, smashed and very finely chopped
- 1 teaspoon capers, drained and very finely chopped
- 2 anchovies, very finely chopped
- 1/2 cup mayonnaise
- 2 teaspoons red wine vinegar
- Juice of 1 lemon
- 3 tablespoons olive paste (available in specialty shops)
- 2 tablespoons water, or as needed

**For the fennel confit:**
- 1 small bulb fennel, trimmed
- 1 tablespoon vegetable oil
- 1 onion, coarsely chopped
- 4 cloves garlic, smashed
- 16-ounce can plum tomatoes, drained and slightly crushed
- 1 tablespoon tomato paste
- Juice of 1 lemon
- 2 tablespoons capers, with some of their liquid
- 1 tablespoon Niçoise olives, pitted and halved
- 1 tablespoon extra-virgin olive oil
- Pinch of granulated sugar

**For the salad:**
- 1/2 pound fine French beans (haricots verts), ends trimmed
- 4 medium red Bliss potatoes, scrubbed
- 1 1/2 pound block of sushi-quality tuna
- Salt and freshly ground pepper
- 1 tablespoon vegetable oil
- 1/2 European cucumber, washed and sliced about 1/8-inch thick (about 1 1/4 cups)
- 1/4 red onion, thinly sliced (about 1/2 cup)
- 2 plum tomatoes, cored and quartered
- 5 cups mesclun salad mixture
- 3 large hard-cooked eggs, peeled and quartered
- Best quality extra-virgin olive oil, for drizzling

Make the tapenade: In a mini-prep or standard food processor, puree the garlic, capers, anchovies, mayonnaise, vinegar, lemon juice, and olive paste until smooth.

Add water a teaspoon or so at a time, processing between each addition, until you have achieved a smooth, vinaigrette consistency. Set aside.

Make the fennel confit: Quarter the fennel lengthwise, through the root, and trim away the tough, triangular core. Cut into 1-inch chunks. Place a large sauté pan over medium heat and add the vegetable oil. When it is very hot, add the fennel, onion and garlic and sauté until golden, 3 to 4 minutes. Add the crushed plum tomatoes and tomato paste, and stir.

Reduce the heat to low and continue to cook for 10 minutes, stirring occasionally, until thickened and almost dry. Stir in the lemon juice, capers, olives, olive oil, and sugar. Stir together, then remove the pan from the heat and let cool.

For the salad: Place a bowl filled with ice and water near the stove. Bring a small pot of generously salted water to a boil and blanch the French beans until tender (not crunchy, but with texture). With a slotted spoon, transfer to the iced water to stop the cooking and preserve the color.

Add the potatoes to the boiling water and cook for about 30 minutes or until tender but not falling apart. Drain, then slice the potatoes into thick slabs.

Season all sides of the block of tuna generously with salt and pepper. Place a large, heavy sauté pan over high heat and add the vegetable oil. When the oil is very hot, add the tuna and sauté for 2 to 3 minutes on each of all 4 sides, depending on how rare you like to serve tuna. Remove from the pan and with a sharp knife, slice the tuna thinly.

In a bowl, toss together the cucumbers, red onion, and tomatoes. Add the mesclun, cooked potatoes, and haricots verts. Season with salt and pepper and drizzle generously with olive oil, then toss gently.

Divide the fennel confit among 4 large plates and top with the salad mixture, making sure each person has an equal ratio of all the ingredients. Arrange the sliced tuna on top of the salads and some of the tapenade vinaigrette over all. Lastly, arrange the quartered hard-cooked eggs on the top, and serve.

# Almond Raspberry Chicken

### Serves 6

2 cups sliced unsalted almonds

2 cups dry breadcrumbs

6 boneless, skinless chicken breasts, pounded slightly to even the thickness

2 cups unbleached all-purpose flour

Salt and freshly ground black pepper

Egg wash (2 large eggs beaten well with ½ cup water)

1 cup apple cider vinegar

1 cup granulated sugar

1 cup chicken stock, preferably homemade

4 ounces fresh or frozen raspberries

Scant ½ teaspoon chipotle paste (on next page)

1 ½ teaspoons cornstarch

3 tablespoons water

¼ cup clarified butter

Fresh raspberries, for garnish

Whole smoked almonds, for garnish

In a food processor, pulse the almonds until coarsely ground. In a large, shallow bowl, combine evenly with the breadcrumbs and set aside.

Place the flour in another shallow bowl, season with 1 teaspoon salt and ½ teaspoon pepper and mix well. Place the egg wash in a third bowl.

Dredge the chicken breasts first in the flour, then the egg wash, and finally in the almond breadcrumbs. Place on a parchment lined baking sheet until ready to cook. (Refrigerate for up to two hours, if desired.)

In a medium saucepan, combine the cider vinegar and sugar and stir together over low heat until the sugar has dissolved. Increase the heat to medium and simmer briskly until reduced by half, about 13 minutes.

Add the chicken stock and the raspberries and simmer for 20 minutes more. The mixture will be thin.

In a small bowl, whisk together the cornstarch and water, and whisk into the sauce. Simmer for 10 minutes more (the sauce will thicken slightly). Remove from heat and whisk in the chipotle paste.

In a large frying pan or skillet, heat the butter over medium-high heat. When it is nice and hot, add and sauté the chicken breasts for 3 to 4 minutes on each side, until golden brown and just firm all the way through (check with a knife if you are not sure when the chicken is fully cooked).

Transfer the chicken breasts to a cutting board and let rest for 2 minutes. Slice on the diagonal and transfer each to a dinner plate, overlapping the slices. Nap each portion with some of the sauce and scatter a few raspberries and smoked almonds over the top.

Serve at once.

Note: To make chipotle paste, place several chipotle peppers en adobo (available in Latin markets and specialty stores) in a small food processor and pulse to a thickish paste.

Butter beans (and all the other shell beans available in the South) make for the most delicious lunch meal. My executive chef, Chuck Taylor, will help himself to a big hot bowl of stewed butter beans with a slice of raw tomato, diced raw red onion and voila, he's got a delicious summer lunch.

— *Nick*

# Smoked Pork Chop, Butter Beans, and Peach Compote

Serves 4

1 cup fresh green butter beans
1 small onion, finely chopped
1/2 carrot, peeled and finely chopped
1 stalk celery, finely chopped
1 small tomato, washed and finely chopped
2 garlic cloves, crushed or finely chopped
2 cups homemade chicken stock or canned low-sodium broth

1 slice bacon, finely chopped
Salt and freshly ground black pepper
4 smoked pork chops
2 tablespoons molasses whisked with 1 teaspoon water
Peach Compote (recipe follows), for serving

To cook the butter beans, place a large saucepan on the stove and in it combine the beans, onion, carrot, celery, tomato, garlic, chicken stock, bacon, and 1 teaspoon salt. Bring to a simmer over medium heat and partially cover the pan. Cook gently for about 30 minutes, until the beans are tender, and set aside.

Preheat an indoor or outdoor grill for medium-high heat cooking. Rub the pork chops all over with the molasses mixture and season both sides with salt and pepper. Grill for 3 minutes, then rotate each chop 45 degrees to create "cross-hatch" marks. Cook for 3 minutes more. Turn the chops over and cook an additional 3 minutes and remove from the heat.

Divide the butter beans, with plenty of their liquid, among the plates. Top with a pork chop, cross-hatch side up, and place a spoonful of peach compote on the side. Serve at once.

# Peach Compote

3 ripe peaches, stoned and cut into 1-inch chunks
1/2 cup granulated sugar
1 tablespoon fresh lemon juice
1 teaspoon finely chopped fresh tarragon leaves
1 tablespoon balsamic vinegar

In a medium saucepan, combine the peaches, lemon juice, and sugar. Place over medium-high heat and stir constantly until the sugar has dissolved. Bring to a boil and allow to boil for 2 minutes. Remove the pan from heat and let cool to room temperature.

Stir in the tarragon and balsamic vinegar, and use as directed.

# Trout with Tomato Lemon Fondue

Serves 4

Tomato Lemon Fondue (recipe follows), for serving
- 2 tablespoons vegetable oil
- Four 8-ounce boneless trout fillets
- Salt and freshly ground black pepper
- 2 pounds baby spinach, triple washed (available at most stores)
- 1 tablespoon extra-virgin olive oil
- Lemon wedges, for serving

Make the Tomato Lemon fondue, if you have not already done so.

Place a large, heavy sauté pan over medium high heat and add the vegetable oil. Season both sides of the trout fillets generously with salt and pepper. When the oil is very hot, sauté the fillets for 2 to 3 minutes on each side, or until lightly brown. Transfer to a warm platter.

Place another sauté pan over high heat and add the olive oil. Add the washed spinach and sauté until just wilted, 1 to 2 minutes. (If desired, prepare the spinach in two batches; wash and dry the pan before sautéing the second batch. Use a total of 1 1/2 tablespoons olive oil, using half for each batch.) Divide the spinach among the dinner plates and top the spinach with a trout fillet. Spoon some of the fondue over the top and place a wedge of lemon on the side of the plate.

# Tomato Lemon Fondue

### Yield: About 1 1/2 cups

2 tablespoons unsalted butter, divided

1 tablespoon extra-virgin olive oil

2 tablespoons finely chopped onion

2 cloves garlic, very finely chopped

2 cups cored, seeded, and 1/4-inch diced fresh tomato
(about 6 medium plum tomatoes)

3 sprigs lemon thyme (if unavailable, substitute regular thyme)

Pinch of granulated sugar

Salt and freshly ground black pepper

Finely chopped zest of one scrubbed lemon

Place a small sauté pan over low heat and add 1 tablespoon of the butter and the olive oil. Add and sweat the onion and garlic, stirring occasionally, until translucent, about 3 minutes. Add the diced tomatoes, lemon thyme, sugar, and salt and pepper to taste. Cook for 5 minutes, stirring occasionally. Add the lemon zest and the remaining 1 tablespoon butter; stir gently for 1 minute and remove from heat. Taste for seasoning and adjust with salt and pepper as necessary.

# Sides

# Fried Green Tomatoes

### Serves 4

2 quarts vegetable oil
2 large, green tomatoes, sliced 1/8-inch thick (about 12 slices)
1 cup Green Tomato Sludge (recipe follows)
1 1/2 cups cornmeal, for dredging
2 large balls fresh mozzarella, sliced 1/8-inch thick (about 8 slices)
Grainy Mustard Sauce, as needed (recipe follows)
2 ounces hard salami, thinly sliced
Baby salad greens, for serving (about 4 ounces)
Equipment: Deep fryer or large, heavy pot; deep-fry thermometer

Preheat the oven to 450°. In a deep-fryer or a large, heavy-based pan, heat
the oil to 350°. Place the sludge in one shallow bowl and the cornmeal in
another. Dredge the tomato slices through the sludge, letting the excess drain
away. Gently dredge in the cornmeal and set the dredged tomatoes on a
parchment-lined baking sheet. Fry the tomatoes in the hot oil for about 2
minutes, until golden and crisp (to avoid overcrowding, fry in two batches,
adding oil as needed for the second batch, or use two pans with the same
amount of oil). With a skimmer or a large slotted spoon, transfer the fried
slices to a paper towel-lined platter (letting the excess oil drain away) while
you fry the remaining tomatoes.

On a lightly oiled baking sheet, stack the tomatoes and mozzarella, starting
and finishing with tomatoes, so each stack contains 3 slices of tomato and 2
slices of mozzarella. Bake for 4 minutes, or until the cheese has just begun to
melt. With a spatula, transfer a stack to each plate. Drizzle each stack with a
little of the mustard sauce and place a slice of salami on top of each stack.
Serve immediately, with a few salad greens on the side of each plate.

# Green Tomato Sludge

### Yield: 1 cup

{
1/4 cup all-purpose flour
3/4 cup buttermilk
2 tablespoons curry powder
1/2 teaspoon cayenne pepper

1/2 tablespoon salt
1/2 teaspoon freshly ground
  black pepper
2 tablespoons water

In a bowl, whisk together all the ingredients until smooth.


# Grainy Mustard Sauce

### Yield: 1 cup

{
1 large egg
1 anchovy
2 cloves garlic, thinly sliced
1/2 teaspoon capers
1 tablespoon Dijon mustard (smooth)
2 tablespoons red wine vinegar
Juice of 1 lemon, about 3 tablespoons

Pinch of grated Parmesan
2 tablespoons extra-virgin olive oil
1/2 cup canola oil
Water as needed
1 1/2 tablespoons whole-grain mustard,
  preferably Pommery
Salt and freshly ground black pepper

In a blender, combine the egg, anchovy, garlic, capers, and Dijon. Blend until smooth, then add the vinegar, lemon juice, and Parmesan and blend again. With the blender running, drizzle in the olive oil and the canola oil very slowly at first, until an emulsion forms. When the mixture is nice and creamy, you can drizzle just a touch faster. Add a teaspoon of water at a time, just until the sauce reaches a spoonable consistency. Transfer to a bowl and stir in the whole-grain mustard; season to taste with salt and pepper. Refrigerate for up to 2 hours (or overnight if desired) before using. (If refrigerated, return to room temperature before serving to allow the flavors to develop.)

# Mashed Potatoes

### Serves 4

3 large Idaho potatoes, about 2 pounds total, washed

8 ounces (2 sticks) unsalted butter, cut into $^1/_2$-inch chunks

$^1/_2$ cup whole milk

$^1/_2$ cup heavy cream

Salt and freshly ground black pepper

Equipment: Moulis (food mill) or ricer for puréeing the potatoes

Peel the potatoes and cut them into large (about 1-inch) pieces. Bring a large pot of salted water to a boil, add the potatoes, and boil until just tender but not falling apart, about 10 minutes.

While the potatoes are cooking, combine the milk and cream in a small pan and warm gently (don't let it boil over!). As soon as the potatoes are done, drain them well and pass through the moulis into a large, warmed bowl. Add the butter and gently stir, then drizzle in the hot cream mixture and stir to combine, just until smooth. Stir in $^1/_2$ teaspoon each of salt and pepper, then taste for seasoning and adjust as necessary. Serve at once.

# Desserts